THE BEGINNER'S GUIDE TO

FB ADVERTISING

I0134929

How to create **effective ads**,
generate leads and increase Your **ROI**

JESSICA AINSWORTH

Contents

An Important Note

Since publishing this book, Facebook has undergone some changes and redesigns. An important one that I feel cannot wait until I release the second edition next year was made to the Business Manager account. You see, Facebook has created what they now call the Business Suite. This also means that some of the links may no longer work. I have double and triple checked this link and at the time of press, this link was in fact working: https://business.facebook.com.

To get to what was formerly called Business Manager, you'll want to click on the "More Tools" option in your Business Suite. Another menu will then appear and from there, you'll want to select "Business Settings".

When we get to the chapter that walks you through setting up your Facebook Business Manager, please refer to the Business Settings webpage. Outside of the new name, all of the functionality remains the same.

For more information regarding the changes between Facebook Business Manager and Facebook Business Suite, please refer to this link:

https://business.facebook.com/business/help/319176852685541

Don't forget to join our Facebook Group to learn more about algorithm updates, changes, etc. in real time.

https://www.facebook.com/groups/FBAdvertisingForBeginners

Sending a BIG shoutout to Jim Henderson for pointing out how confusing this change is when reading the book as a beginner advertiser, which ultimately drove my decision to add this portion in immediately.

In fact, I may release the second edition earlier than planned and am aiming for Spring of 2021 - so be on the lookout!

And as always, thank you for your support and for reading my book. Writing this book was my way of helping business owners. If you see something wrong or would like something clarified or added, please send me a message on Facebook (https://www.facebook.com/PendragonConsultingLLC) or post in our Facebook Group and I'd be happy to clarify and possibly add it to the second edition to ensure that we're addressing all concerns and questions!

Acknowledgements

It takes a village….

Have you ever heard the saying, "It takes a village?" As much as I'd like to take credit for this book all on my own, I would be remiss if I didn't say that I had a village to support me.

To my husband and kids for listening to me grumble and read aloud. For all of the time, they've sacrificed so I could finish my book. For the pile of dishes that, if I ignored long enough while trying to get the next chapter hammered out, would magically clean by themselves. I will be ever grateful to all of them for the love and encouragement when I was at my worst. And for listening to me grumble… again.

Thank you to Sherry and Bob for stepping in and helping with my children when I had deadlines to meet. I can't tell you how much I love and appreciate you guys!

To my awesome friends that have been a beacon of support.

To Steve and Jyllian, founders of Precision Legal Marketing, who have been the most amazing mentors ever. Do you know the saying that there's a difference between bosses and leaders? They are undoubtedly leaders. They treat their employees amazingly, go out of the way for their clients, and are freaking rock stars at law firm marketing.

To all of you reading this book, thank you for your support!

Download Your FREE Gifts!

We've put together some resources to help you implement your Facebook Advertising strategy. From templates to worksheets and infographics, you'll find a ton of resources to help you take the next step. To access the free resources mentioned in this book (and more!), simply follow the link below.

Download your FREE resources here:

https://www.beginnersguidetomarketing.com/facebookadvertising

Check out our website for additional resources, information and upcoming books:

www.beginnersguidetomarketing.com

Introduction

There is a world of possibilities out there when it comes to social media marketing. Although, the landscape has evolved, branched, and become somewhat more sophisticated in the last few years, the opportunity of connecting and engaging with a loyal audience remains a highlight.

With more than 2.6 billion monthly active users around the world, Facebook has truly become a Goliath in terms of social media platforms. Even with Instagram (now owned by Facebook), Twitter, and "trendy" platforms such as Vine, Musical.ly/TikTok, Facebook has been able to sustain its position at the top. Hence, Facebook is more popular among both personal and business users compared to other social media platforms.

Considering the sheer number of people from all walks of life having a Facebook account is common, it has become an important and essential part of the business's overall social media strategy. The cost of lost opportunities by *not* being on Facebook is high.

In the words of none other than the brains behind Facebook, Mark Zuckerberg:

"Think about what people are doing on Facebook all day. They're keeping up with their friends and family, but they're also building an image and identity for themselves, which in a sense is their brand. They're connecting with the audience that they want to connect to. It's almost a disadvantage if you're not on it now."

Adding a Layer of the COVID-19 Pandemic

It was the 11th of March in 2020 when the rapidly worsening Novel Coronavirus finally declared as a *pandemic* by the World Health Organization (WHO). Since then, the situation has been developing at an increasingly rapid rate – and not necessarily in a positive way.

With strict nation-wide lockdowns racking the economies of many nations, social distancing, and stringent operating procedures and regulations imposed on "essential services" and other businesses, there has been a lot of disturbance in the economy.

According to a CNBC article published in April, more than 7.5 small businesses risk permanent closures and further stymieing if the pandemic-related disruption continues worsening.

In this scenario, many small businesses have turned to adopt new cost-cutting procedures, which includes reducing spend on conventional marketing and turning to the powers of Facebook advertising.

However, considering that many of these businesses don't have the funds (or quite honestly, the time and desire) to work with marketing/advertising agencies, they have decided to wing it and conduct Facebook advertising on their own.

While there is no doubt that there are many multi-talented business owners that can do it, others lack the skills to fine-tune the details to produce optimal results. The example below puts the weight of this in perspective.

The Pizza Place Targeting Debacle

There's a pizzeria here in Maryland that took the self-Facebook-advertising route to let people know they are offering free delivery and curbside pickup for the duration of the lockdown.

The problem here is that they are 3 hours away from me, but I can still see their advertisement. This means that they have not clearly defined their target audience and are not effectively spending their budget. I, being hours away, am not their ideal customer.

After messaging them about this, they confessed that they were new to Facebook advertising and didn't know what they were doing. As a result, they had set the geo-tag for the entire country.

Without fixing their location, this would lead to some very disappointed customers at the other end of the country, and their return on investment (ROI) would be minimal.

Other Complications

On top of the COVID-19 pandemic, another major issue small businesses ignore is the difference between organic and paid advertisements.

To sum it up, organic reach refers to the audience you can attract and gain simply with just the posts you make, i.e. no money spent. The twist is that with increased competition and continuous growth of the platform, organic reach is declining. Thanks to Facebook's algorithm updates in recent years, you can expect your organic posts to reach between 1.6% - 2% of your page's followers.

This is why marketers choose to boost advertisements with payment, so more people in their chosen target would see it and hopefully convert to a qualified sales lead.

Businesses need to understand the nuances of these differences to truly master Facebook advertisements for themselves.

The purpose of this book is to teach such aspiring marketers the art of Facebook advertising. We'll dip into what it is, how you can begin, and a few tips to increase your ROI, conversion rates, and cost-effectiveness.

We will take the journey from developing the campaign to playing it out in this guide.

Facebook Advertisement – Peeking into Possibilities

The What

The point of this guide is to uncomplicate things for the average Facebook advertiser. With that taken into account, the simplest way to describe a Facebook ad is anything you see on your News Feed. They are like regular ads promoting your business, just exclusively on Facebook and Instagram. Facebook owns Instagram, and you can choose whether or not to have your ad shown on Instagram as well as Facebook when setting up your ad, but we'll get to that later.

The Facebook algorithm – essentially a proverbial cog that makes the world of Facebook advertising go round – helps businesses reach their targeted audience. Targeting is the main element here that enables you to define your potential audience using location, demographics, and other profiling insights.

The Why

The "why" is quite simple to understand – 2.6 billion active users!

With such a large population using this platform, businesses have the opportunity to maximize their reach and increase conversion rates.

Furthermore, the wide range of options for customizing and targeting advertisements, businesses have more creative control over their advertisements. You also have the ability to sync the ads with your Instagram ads to create a multi-platform campaign and enhance your reach.

Facebook Ads also give you access to metrics and analytics; you can track to see how your ads perform. For example, you can track your reach, the number of clicks, Cost per Click or CPC, and Cost per Conversion, etc.

This will help you determine whether you're earning an ROI that is profitable to your business or whether you need to make some changes for better targeting.

The gist of it is the fact that Facebook is too big, powerful, and continuously evolving a platform to ignore. From small businesses with hyper-localized audiences to multinational B2B companies with clientele all around the world, the opportunities for reaching a large audience is highly profitable.

The How

Overall, more than 3 million businesses of all sizes use Facebook ads – with 70% of these businesses being located outside of the United States. While the management and monitoring process for each of these businesses is different, they all begin by setting up a Facebook Business page.

Once the page is set up, you would then make your way to the Facebook Business Manager and through there, the Ads Manager to begin (we'll go step by step in the next few chapters). While it's very easy (and tempting) to simply "boost a post" direct from your Facebook business page, it is not as likely to have a high ROI. If you're looking to simply boost the engagement level of your page or attract some new followers, then boosting the post may be the right option for you. However, for attracting sales leads, you'll achieve your optimal results by creating your ads through Facebook Business Manager.

To help you even more along your journey through Facebook Advertising, we've created some free resources that are available for you to download at:

http://www.beginnersguidetomarketing.com/facebookadvertising

We've also created a Facebook Group to bring together a like-minded community of individuals focused on tips, tricks, strategies and valuable resources to take your Facebook Advertising even further. Join today at:

https://www.facebook.com/groups/FBAdvertisingForBeginners/

What You Need to Get Started

Getting started with Facebook Advertising can be a relatively simple process, made even easier with our step by step instructions. So, without further ado, here's what you need to get started with advertising on Facebook:

1. Facebook User Profile
2. Facebook Business Page
3. Business Manager Account
4. Billing Setup
5. An Understanding of Your Target Audience
6. Instagram Account (Optional)
7. Facebook Pixel (Recommended)

Facebook User Profile

It's hard to deny that an enormous amount of people are on Facebook. You know this; we know this - that's why you're reading this book because you understand the power it holds for advertising and reaching a large audience.

If you're one of the few individuals left without a Facebook profile (seriously, do you live under a rock?! I kid, I kid), then read on to learn how to set up your personal profile. In order to create a business page on Facebook, you'll need to have a personal profile. For those who already have a personal profile, feel free to skip this section and move on to the next step.

To create your free profile on Facebook, visit https://www.facebook.com. You'll need to enter your name, email address or phone number, password, birthday, and gender. Once you've done all of that, you'll need to verify your account by either email or phone.

That's it. All done. Now, you're free to add any other information, a profile picture and cover photo, update your privacy settings (we strongly recommend that!), etc. Once you've finished getting your personal profile set up the way you'd like, hop on over to the next step.

Facebook Business Page

In this section, we're going to walk-through how-to setup your business page and run through the basics. The next section will focus on how to really optimize your business page to make sure your page is both professional and quality.

There are two ways in which you can get to the Pages page. First, you can either type in https://www.facebook.com/pages to take you there directly (you must be signed into Facebook), or you can click on the "Pages" tab on the left-side menu of your News Feed.

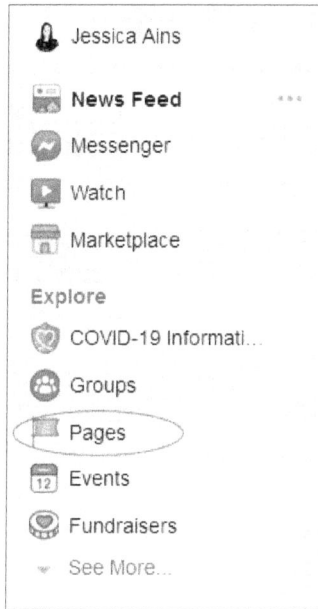

Figure-01

Once you're on the page, click on "Create Page" at the top right of the page. Next, you'll need to select your page type. Are you a brand or business? Or are you a community or public figure?

After you've determined the correct type of page, you get to select your page name and category. What best describes your page?

Save it and boom, that's it. Now, you can go in and add your business' contact information, cover and profile photo, about, etc. The next chapter is on optimizing your Facebook business page, which can walk you through setting your page up for success.

Facebook Business Manager

This section is literally just setting up your Business Manager. We'll do a walkthrough of Facebook Business Manager in the next couple of chapters, so hold tight, and baby step it.

You can sign up for your Business Manager account by visiting https://www.business.facebook.com.

Billing Setup

You will not be able to run any ads until you've connected a payment method in your Ads Manager account.

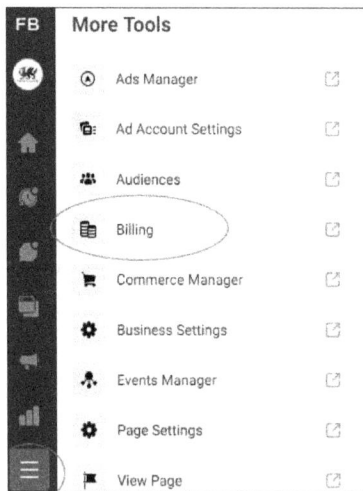

Figure-02

There are two ways in which to get to the place in which you'll need to enter your payment method. First, you can visit https://www.facebook.com/ads/manager/

account_settings/account_billing, or you can click on "More Tools" from the left-side menu in business manager, followed by "billing".

From here, you'll want to click on "Payment Settings" on the top right of the page. In here, you can enter or edit your payment information as well as control your spending limit and view all of your receipts from prior payments (←that's handy come tax time).

Now, let's get to optimizing your Facebook business page to get it all spiffy and professional before we start advertising your brand and page.

Defining Your Target Audience

Not everyone is your customer.

"Why do I need to define an audience?"

The answer is simple. In order to lead a successful marketing campaign, you must understand who you're marketing to. Knowing who your target audience is can help determine where the best place to market to them is and knowing this could save you big bucks!

If you're selling a baby product, you may not be looking to market to those who don't have children. If you're selling a service geared towards those in their 20's to 30's, you don't want to waste your hard-earned money on marketing to everyone from 13 - 65+. Understanding this can save you money and help you develop a marketing strategy for success.

In mid-March of 2020, many states had issued executive orders closing non-essential businesses and ordering a shelter in place. Business owners were swept up in the whirlwind of everything, wondering how their business would survive an extended closure. Without customers, how could they pay their employees who were depending on their income? Without generating revenue, would they even be able to pay their rent for their shops?

Many businesses turned to find creative ways to stay afloat. My husband and I enjoy paint night date nights, and our favorite place creatively dreamed up cabin fever kits that included everything you'd need for a paint night at home. We were ecstatic that we could continue to have date nights - after the kids went to bed, of course. You see, we have three small children, so the big paint night chains offering virtual paint nights weren't feasible for us, as they typically began at around 5 or 6 in the evening, which is when we feed the kids dinner, bathe them and start to settle for the evening. However, recognizing an opportunity, this paint night chain had capitalized and created the cabin fever kits. I know we're not the only parents out there grateful for date night kits we could enjoy at our leisure. It was through recognizing that at least a portion of their target audience were parents or others who were unable to enjoy the virtual sessions that they found some success.

Restaurants aren't exempt from this. Kids are out of school - in many states until at least May. These kids have had their lives turned upside down with new school routines (IF school has continued for them), not able to play with their friends or go anywhere. Even parks have been closed down. Many restaurants have recognized this and created some really fun family meal packs. Some of our favorites are the "kits" these restaurants, particularly the pizzerias, have put together - these come with dough,, sauce and all the toppings for your kids to play chef and make their own pizzas. As a parent, I absolutely LOVE this. We've even had some local bakers create some sugar cookie kits with pre-baked cookies and a couple of different packs of frosting and sprinkles for you to decorate. We found this particularly exciting around Easter.

Don't worry I'm definitely going somewhere with this and not just rattling on about some of the things we enjoyed during the quarantine. It was through innovation and recognizing a need within their target audiences that these businesses were able to at least generate some income.

Many businesses have turned to advertising on social media to let their potential customers know that they were still open and maybe to showcase some of their selections - or even to announce a new product such as the pizza kits or cabin fever paint kits. However, without a clear idea of who their target audience is, it's easy for a business to target the wrong people. Let's look at another example.

One day, not long after businesses were forced close, an advertisement for a pizzeria came across my news feed on Facebook. They were offering free delivery within a certain radius, and I was on board with potentially ordering from them. However, when I went to their Facebook page, I was surprised to discover that they were a little over two hours north of me. Being well outside the radius and in fact far enough away from them to tell that I'm most definitely NOT their ideal customer, I messaged their page to let them know they should consider tightening up their geographic targeting on their advertisement. After offering to assist them, they had confessed that they had been accidentally targeting the entire United States!

I have no idea how long they had been running that advertisement, but I do know that they wasted money on targeting the wrong people. You see, without a clear understanding of who you should be marketing your company to (and the tools that you're using), it's easy to fall down the trap of wasting money. As a business owner, you want to spend your hard-earned money on producing qualified leads for your sales team that eventually convert to paying customers. At the end of the day, that's what we all want.

Here's another reason why ensuring that you're producing content geared at your target audience is important. Perhaps you're paying to advertise to the wider audience just to boost engagements and build a following, but these people are not likely to convert to paying customers. Not only is this a waste of your money, but it also affects the algorithm for advertising campaigns. That last part is especially important if you're using tracking for retargeting purposes through Google Ads or the Facebook Pixel. Those unqualified leads are then captured in your spider web, and you'll continue wasting your money on any retargeting efforts.

The more you understand just who your target audience is, the more you'll also understand where your ideal customers are and the kind of content that will resound better with them. People who are not in your target audience may still buy from you. In fact, you can still sell to them. Your target audience revolves around those who are most likely to make a purchase and, therefore, are your targeted audience.

All right. Enough about why defining your target audience is important. Now onto how you can define your target audience. As we go through this, please keep in mind that it's always a good practice to periodically check to ensure your target audience remains the same. COVID-19 presented volatile, unprecedented times that will have a lasting impact. Consumer behaviors have changed drastically after the pandemic took us by storm. In 2008, the economy was rocked by the housing market and the ensuing stock market crash and subsequent recession. These major events should force business owners to take a look at their target audience as it may change at a rapid pace and continue to evolve as the economy recovers.

That's right, ladies and gentlemen you can't escape economics.

So, how do we define our target audiences? Many business owners make the mistake of following their gut instinct and not doing the research. With a little bit of research on your audience, you'll find a higher return on investment on your marketing efforts. What should you be researching? It's tempting to come in with a group of people that you'd like to market to, but that's not always the right answer. Let's start by looking at your current customers. That may be easier said than done for those who have been in business for a little while. Those just starting out should take a look at their closest competitors.

Use this list as a starting point to help you determine commonalities in your current customers:

- Age
- Location
- Language
- Spending Power
- Jobs/Careers/Positions
- Interests
- Stage of Life

Not all of those demographics will be relevant for your business. If you're in retail, the jobs/careers/positions may not be relevant.

Age will be relevant for most industries, if not all. For example, a divorce lawyer is not going to be targeting minors - or likely even those between 18 - 25. We're not saying that some adults between the ages of 18 - 25 aren't going to be looking for a divorce lawyer. What we're saying is that the average age of those seeking divorces is typically higher, and therefore, that age group should be excluded from the lawyer's target audience.

Many companies offer products or services to clients within specific geographic regions. Even for those whose clients come from all over the U.S., you likely have higher concentrations of clients in particular areas.

Have you ever heard some people say, "You know what the word assume means, right? It means to make an A$$ out of U and ME." Well, language is an area that many (including myself at one point) have a common misconception that if you're in the U.S., your audience speaks English. We are a melting pot of diversity. Assuming that your target audience solely speaks English is wrong. This is why research is so important.

Spending power and ultimately, income are areas that some businesses will need to take into account. A customer with a lower-income level may not have as large of a disposable income. It doesn't mean that customers in this category should be excluded from your target audience if they are your most likely customer. Again, we come back to relevancy for some businesses. For industries such as wealth management and real estate, spending power and income levels will be more relevant.

Jobs/Careers/Positions is another demographic that may not be as relevant for every business. However, for those targeting a B2B market or again, industries such as the financial sector who may be targeting wealthy entrepreneurs, this demographic can be key.

What do your customers like to do (aside from enjoying your products and services)? What other businesses do they frequent or follow on social media? We're not telling you to go out there and stalk your clients, but their interests and pastimes can help you further define where you should be marketing to your target audience as well as what kind of content may resonate better with them.

Finally, we come to the stage of life demographic. Are you customers likely to be college students? New parents (remember those paint nights and pizza kits)? Getting ready to retire? Already retired?

Yet another useful way to help determine your target audience is by reviewing your social media business pages. They all offer an "insights" tab that shows you the numbers and analytics behind your page. How active is your page? Have you acquired any new followers? Who is interacting and engaging with your page? Knowing this information can help you fill in the knowledge gaps to further refine your audience.

Now, we briefly mentioned a little earlier that conducting a competitor analysis can help you identify your potential clients as well. Using those same guidelines, we talked about above, have a look at who your competitors are targeting and who their current clients are. Innovation can help set you apart, but knowing what's already working and what's not can provide some much-needed information to get you started. The caveat here is that you won't be able to get a detailed analysis of your competitors' clients and those interacting with their social pages, but again, it's a good jumping-off point.

Make a statement. While we won't go into how to write

a brand positioning statement in this book, you should consider making a statement that will define your target audience. Take a look at some of your favorite brand's positioning statements. We'll look at Nike's brand positioning statement, for example:

> "For serious athletes, Nike gives confidence that provides the perfect shoe for every sport."

Phil Knight and Bill Bowerman, the founders of the Nike brand, were they themselves athletes who had recognized a hole in the market. Bill Bowerman, a famous track and field coach, set out to increase running speed by decreasing the weight of the shoe.

> "A shoe must be three things; It must be light, comfortable, and it's got to go the distance." - Bill Bowerman.

They developed their brand with a target audience in mind, but their brand has since evolved into more than just producing shoes for runners. What did you notice about their positioning statement? They've identified their target audience as being serious athletes.

Some final advice on establishing your target audience (and connecting it with content marketing) is this: Be willing to make mistakes. Nothing is ever really cut and dry. You're going to make mistakes; we all make mistakes - even this author. Don't get hung up on one particular idea. If something is working, remain flexible and open-minded until you find what resonates with your target audience.

You always have the option to do some A/B split testing to determine what wording or which images may invoke a stronger response from your target audience, but it all starts with defining exactly who you're targeting.

Feel free to use the worksheet we put together to help you stay organized while you're doing your research.

Optimizing Your Facebook Business Page

There are over 2.6 billion monthly active users on Facebook… does your company have a business page?

With over 2.6 billion users, can your business afford to NOT be on Facebook? Building a business page on the popular social media platform is a great way to reach new potential customers - for free. That's right; it's free to create a business page on Facebook. Take your social media marketing to the next level and build a page optimized for success.

Facebook pages help your brand or business promote and share value-added content as well as to assist in customer support. Did you know that two-thirds of U.S. adults report they use Facebook with a whopping 74% of users reporting that they check Facebook *daily*?!

Set yourself up for success on Facebook with these simple steps.

Manage Roles

As a business owner you may want to add team members to help manage your Facebook Business Page. To add team members or edit their roles, simply open the Settings tab from your Business page. From here, click on the tab called Page Roles from the left-side menu.

At the top of the page, you'll see three options: Assign a new page role, page owner and existing page roles. To add a new team member to your Business Page, simply choose the first option. You can use the search bar under that option to look them up to be either their name or email address.

The roles you can assign to your team members are:

- Admin - Full access
- Editor - Publish content, send Messenger messages, respond and delete comments, create ads, see who posted and view Insights
- Moderator - Send Messenger messages, respond and delete comments, see who posted and view Insights
- Advertiser - Create ads, see who posted and view Insights
- Analyst - Can view who posted and the Insights
- Custom - Must be defined in Business Manager

If you're working with an agency, you may need to assign them the role of Page Owner for them to be able to create ads for you.

If you'd like to edit the roles of existing team members, you can do so in the Existing Page Roles section a bit further down the page.

6 Steps to Optimizing Your Facebook Business Page

1. Select the right type of page
2. Custom username
3. Images
4. Fill out all of your details - Don't leave any blanks!
5. Ensure your contact information is accurate
6. Remove/hide unused tabs

Select the Right Type of Page

When you first create your Facebook business page, you'll be able to choose from a variety of options such as:

- Local business or place
- Company
- Brand or Product
- Public Figure
- Entertainment
- Cause or Community

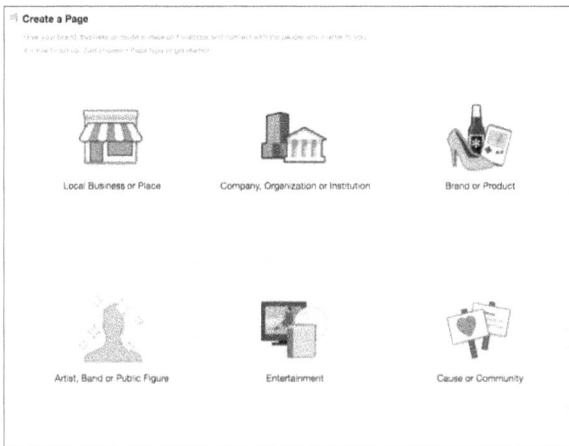

Figure-3

By selecting the right type of page from the onset, it can help enhance the way you communicate the message that your company wishes to show.

Create a Custom Username

You have the ability to create your own username. For instance, on Facebook, the Pendragon username is @

pendragonconsultingllc (so, go follow us!). However, if you'd like something different or want it to match other social accounts who don't offer the ability to be choosy, you do have some flexibility there. We've noticed in some cases that those who don't create a username for their page just don't end up with one at all. So, make sure that you've checked the box and create a custom username for your business page, so you don't end up with a random string of alphanumeric characters for your Facebook slug.

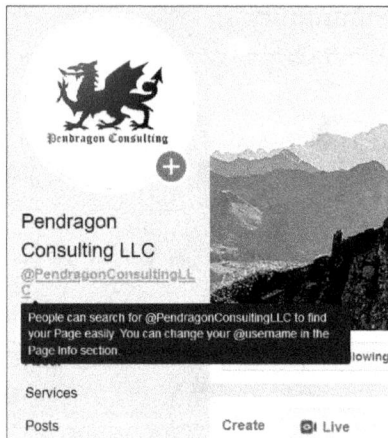

Figure-4

Images

All right. Now, what picture should you post for your business? Your hot new product? The CEO of your company? A staff photo? Logo? While the answer may differ depending on your brand and industry, the majority of businesses favor using their logo. This can really help you create brand awareness and brand recognition for your company. The trick to your profile and the cover image is consistency. Again, in an effort to foster brand recognition and brand awareness, you want to present a consistent brand across your digital marketing efforts such as social media platforms and on your website.

Fill Out All Your Details - Don't Leave Any Blanks!

All right. This is one of the most common issues we run across when we take over the social media marketing for our clients - either missing or inaccurate information throughout their Facebook business page. Ensure that you input as much as you can into your profile, such as your contact information, set your categories (what industry are you in?), your about section, "our story," and even your open hours. Not only does this help users find you easier, but it also helps to instill confidence in the fact that you're a professional organization, not taking a half-hearted approach. Incomplete or inaccurate profiles may be a negative sign to potential buyers, indicating that you cut corners (though not always).

Ensure Your Contact Information is Accurate

This is not only important so that your potential customers can find you, but also for local SEO purposes. Counting as a directory listing (aka citation), you want to ensure you have accurate information to promote your local SEO and to avoid being downranked. If Google or the other search engines aren't clear on your correct contact information so as to provide accurate information to their users, they may end up downranking your website.

Remove/Hide Unused Tabs

While you won't have the ability to turn off *all* of the tabs, you do have the ability to turn off a bunch of them. If they're not relevant and/or you're not using them, turn them off, so they don't appear on your business page. Just one step closer to having that spiffy, professional page that demonstrates your brand's level of quality.

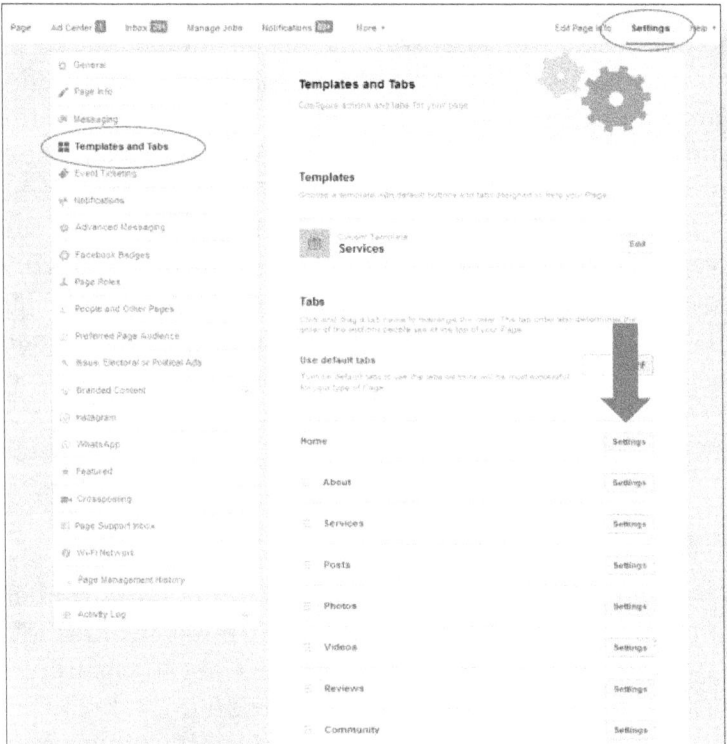

Figure-5

Linking Instagram to Your Facebook Page

Now owned by Facebook, Instagram is yet another free social networking site for you to capitalize on. You have the ability to simultaneously post to both Facebook and Instagram by linking your accounts. You can accomplish this by click on Settings from your Facebook Business Page and then clicking on Instagram on the left side menu.

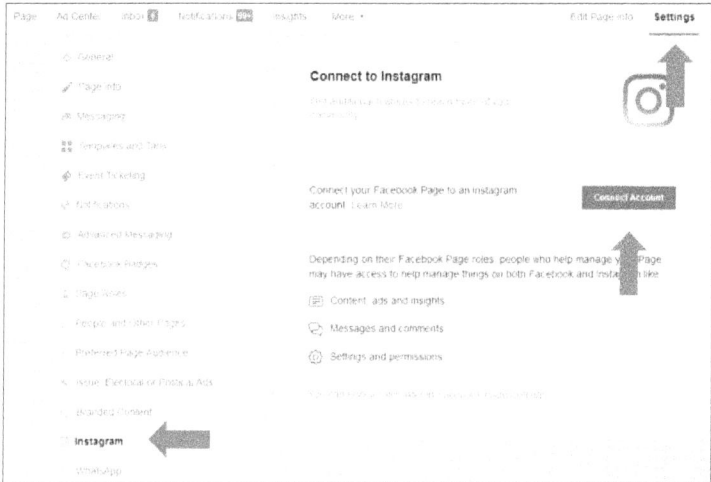

Figure-6

Once you've clicked on the Instagram tab, click on the blue button labeled "Connect Account." During this process, you'll be asked to provide your username and password to login to your Instagram account in order to establish the connection. You may also be asked to upgrade to a business account as many people sign-up initially as individuals and not businesses. That's it. It's really just that simple.

Understanding Facebook Insights

When advertising on Facebook, you'll have two batches on Insights you can rely on. The first, which we'll cover more here, is the Insights tab located on your Business Page. The second is the Insights tab that is connected to your Facebook Pixel.

This is a free tool and it allows you to understand some of the basics - such as whether you've added any new followers, what your typical reach and engagement levels are, etc. The Overview tab that is the first screen to show is not all you can see though.

While you can gain a great understanding of the flow of your page from here, one of the things I find most helpful is the tab called Posts in Insights. This shows you which days and times of the week are the most engaging and when your dead zones are. You can use this information to help you with your dayparting. We cover this a bit more in-depth in the chapter on dayparting.

Of course, you'll be able to access similar information from your Business Manager. In Business Manager's Insights, you'll be able to see Insights for both Facebook and Instagram. You can see the gender and age breakdown of your followers, what country they come from, your most engaging content, along with some trends in your content flow.

Facebook Business Manager

Facebook Business Manager is the hub for your advertising needs, but ultimately, there's so much more that you can do from there.

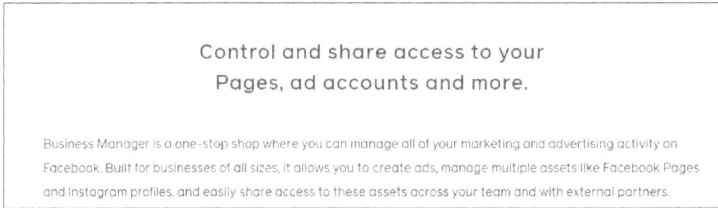

> ## Control and share access to your Pages, ad accounts and more.
>
> Business Manager is a one-stop shop where you can manage all of your marketing and advertising activity on Facebook. Built for businesses of all sizes, it allows you to create ads, manage multiple assets like Facebook Pages and Instagram profiles, and easily share access to these assets across your team and with external partners.

Figure-7

In addition to creating and managing your ads, you can also control and manage access and permissions for assets associate with your business manager all in one place. Additionally, you can maintain a certain level of privacy by working with your colleagues through Business Manager instead of having to add them to your personal Facebook account to grant them access.

We walked you through how to set up your Business Manager account in a previous chapter. So, let's dive into all things related to Facebook Business Manager.

Adding People to Your Account

If you're working with others on creating ads, maintaining Facebook pages and all that jazz, you'll want to add people to your Business Manager account. There are two main categories in which you would add an individual to your account, and they are Business Admins who can control all aspects of Business Manager and Business Employees who cannot see all of the assets in business settings, but rather only make changes to the individual assets that you've granted them access to.

Another option out there is called the Granting Partner Access option and is for those who are working with a third party, such as an agency or vendor.

Further, as you get more into the weeds of things and your company really takes off (if it hasn't already), you may need to add some other, more advanced options in the finance realm. You're able to grant access as either a Finance Analyst or Finance Editor to your Business Manager account.

Once you've added individuals to your Business Manager account, you can then begin the task of granting permissions. You can allow them permission to access your business's assets in Business Settings - such as ad accounts, Pages, pixels and/or catalogs.

Let's say that you wanted to allow someone to post to the page and not be able to create or manage any ads - you're able to toggle permissions for each individual you've invited to work on your Business Manager.

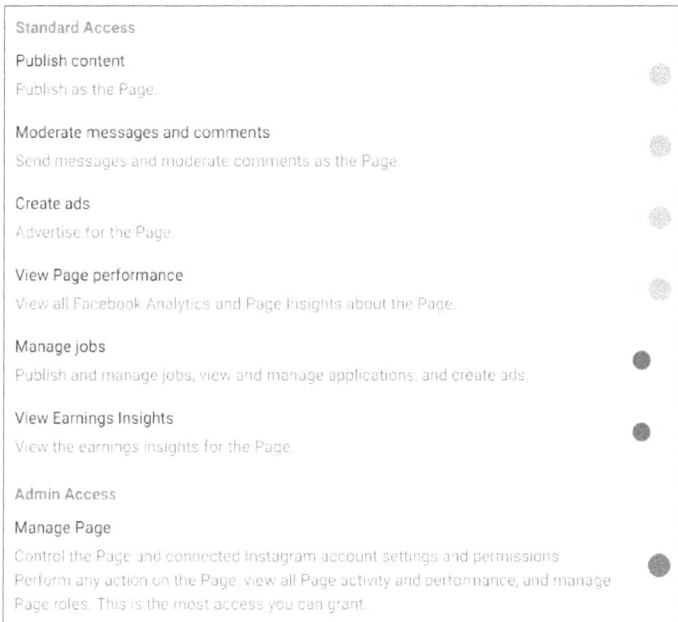

Figure-8

To add someone to your Business Manager account, you would choose Business Settings from the left-side menu, followed by the first option in the left-side menu called Users and then People. Partners are where you would add your third-party vendors or agencies.

Click on the blue "Add" button to add an individual to your Business Manager account. A popup will open prompting you to enter the person's email address along with assigning them either a business or finance role:

- Employee Access - limited/restricted access
- Admin Access - full access
- Financial Analyst - view financial details

- Finance Editor - edit and view financial details and accounts

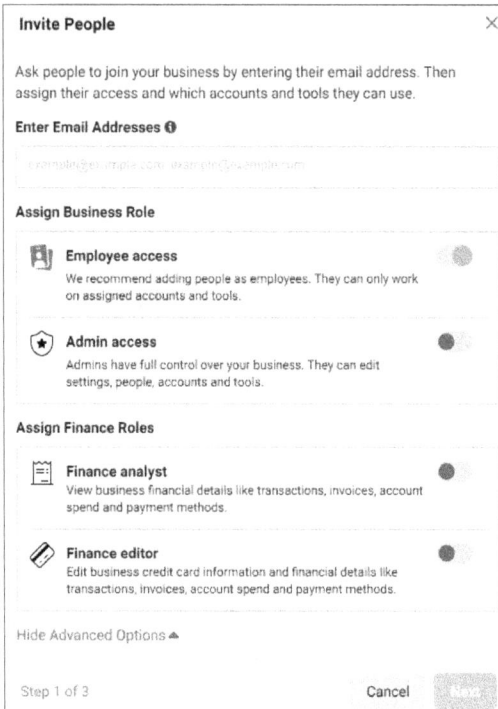

> **Invite People**   ×
>
> Ask people to join your business by entering their email address. Then assign their access and which accounts and tools they can use.
>
> **Enter Email Addresses** ❶
>
> _____
>
> **Assign Business Role**
>
> 🔲 **Employee access**
> We recommend adding people as employees. They can only work on assigned accounts and tools.
>
> ⭐ **Admin access**
> Admins have full control over your business. They can edit settings, people, accounts and tools.
>
> **Assign Finance Roles**
>
> 📋 **Finance analyst**
> View business financial details like transactions, invoices, account spend and payment methods.
>
> ✏️ **Finance editor**
> Edit business credit card information and financial details like transactions, invoices, account spend and payment methods.
>
> Hide Advanced Options ▲
>
> Step 1 of 3   Cancel   Next

Figure-9

If you've set them as an Employee, you'll need to decide which pages and accounts you'd like them to have access to and what specific accesses they'll be granted. For instance, do you want them to be able to create ads, but not be able to moderate comments? They'll need to accept access on their end as the final step.

Creating an Ad Account

Before you can get started creating advertisements, you'll need to have an Ad account setup. At this stage, you should have added a payment method in your billing. The next step is to set up your Ad account in the Business Manager. You'll do this by clicking on Business Settings on the left-side menu, followed by Ad Accounts under the "Accounts" dropdown menu.

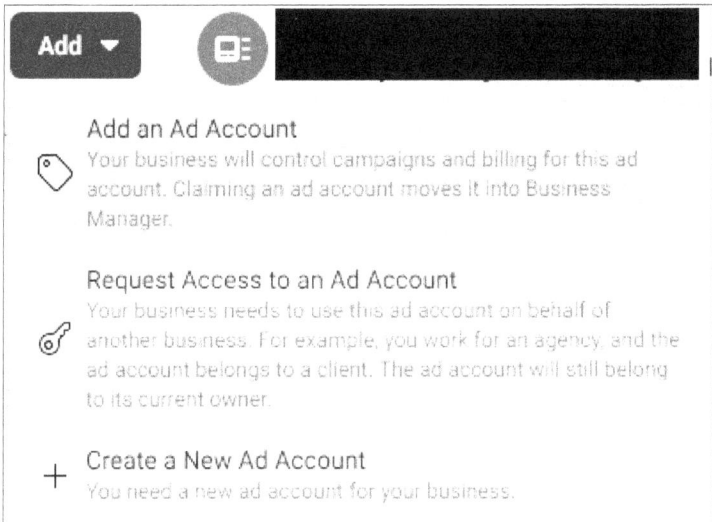

Figure-10

Click on the "Add" button and select the appropriate option. To set up an ad account to a Facebook Page, you must be the Page *owner*. This setting can be updated from your Facebook Page's settings.

In the ad account section, you'll be able to edit your ad account name, time zone, currency, advertising purpose, tax ID and business address. Bear in mind that if you select the wrong time zone, your ads will be displayed based on the wrong time zone and could impact your ROI.

Linking Your Instagram Account

That's right. Facebook owns LinkedIn, and if you wanted to run Instagram ads through your Facebook Business Manager, you need to link your accounts. In the Business Settings on your Business Manager account, you'll see Instagram Accounts under the Accounts dropdown on the left-side menu.

The next step would be to click on "Add," just like you did to add an ad account, and you'll be prompted to connect your Instagram account, which will require signing in.

After your Instagram account has been successfully added, you can assign partners and, more importantly, Add Assets. Add Assets is where you would add your Ad account to your Instagram account. Again, if the ad account isn't connected to your Instagram account, you won't be able to advertise on Instagram from the Business Manager/Ads Manager. You must have your ad account set up prior to adding it to your Instagram account.

Speaking of adding an Instagram account... don't forget to follow us on Instagram (and Facebook).

Data Sources

In this tab on the Business Settings menu, you'll be able to view any pixels you have installed. You can also click on the Events Manager button of your pixel to view real-time data, analytics and the health of your pixel (sometimes you may need to troubleshoot your pixel). If you're not sure whether your pixel is working, you'll be able to test out the functionality of your pixel in the Events Manager as well. This provides some excellent insights as to what's happening on your website. (Though Google Analytics is better - this author is partial!)

You can also set up and manage your Offline Events such as call tracking and other sources. You can also attach your ad account to this data source in addition to adding people and editing their permissions.

Brand Safety

From here, you'll be able to add the domains of your partners as well as manage your block list. You have the ability to block certain apps or pages from displaying your advertisement. To do this, you'll need to first identify which apps or pages you'd like to block, and you can do this by downloading the Publisher List (also in Brand Safety). The Publisher List is a list of where your ad may be displayed for the Audience Network, Instant Articles and Instream Videos. This can be particularly important if you're looking to avoid having your advertisements shown on specific websites, articles or video streams.

Another key feature of Brand Safety is that you're able to see exactly where your ads have been shown. For instance, if you've run an ad and allowed placement in the Audience Network, your ad may have been shown on the *Words with Friends* app (yes, that is one of Facebook's partners in the Audience Network).

Integrations

When you go into a tab called Leads Access under Integrations in the left-side menu of your Business Settings, you can connect your CRM. Facebook allows you to connect one of the following CRM platforms to your Business Manager account:

- HubSpot
- Infusionsoft
- Salesforce
- Zoho CRM

By connecting your CRM platform to your Business Manager, you help simplify your lead generation process in that any leads generated through Facebook can automatically be sent to your CRM. If you use anything outside of the listed CRM platforms, you can always request a new partner be added to the integrations list.

Registrations

If you'd like your articles to be eligible for Instant Articles, you must register your news pages to Facebook. In order to register your account to be eligible for Instant Articles, you'll need to add your website, verify your domain, verify your business and register content behind paywalls (if you have a hard paywall, you'll need to provide Facebook with your paywall test credentials or whitelist Facebook's user agent.)

Once you submit your request for eligibility, you can also go in and add your logo as well as links to any policies your website may have, such as a fact-checking policy, ethics policy, etc.

Other Partner Integrations

CRM platforms aren't the only integration you can link your Facebook Business Manager to. Check out the list below, and remember that you can always request a new partner be added by Facebook and that while we intend this book to be updated annually, in the time, it takes to write and release this book, there may have been some updates/changes to partners.

- CRM and Marketing
  - HubSpot
  - Infusionsoft
  - Salesforce
  - Zoho CRM

- E-commerce
  - 3dcart
  - BigCommerce
  - Ecwid
  - Eventbrite
  - Magento
  - OpenCart
  - PrestaShop
  - Shopify
  - Storeden
  - Ticketmaster
  - WooCommerce

- Mobile Platforms
  - AppsFlyer
  - Adjust
  - Branch
  - Kochava
  - mParticle

- Singular
- Offline Conversions
  - Segment
  - Zapier
- Tag Management
  - Google Tag Manager
- Website
  - Bandzoogle
  - Drupal
  - Jimdo
  - Joomla
  - Kajabi
  - Segment
  - Shopline
  - Squarespace
  - Teespring
  - Webflow
  - Wix
  - WordPress

The Facebook Pixel

If you are presently using Facebook ads or are planning to use it in the future, there is one vital tool you should start using right away - the Facebook Pixel. It will allow you to reap the most benefits out of your social ad budget.

Read on to learn all about Facebook Pixel and how it works.

What is Facebook Pixel?

The Facebook Pixel is simply a code that is placed on a website to collect data and helps to build a target audience for future ads, track conversions from existing Facebook ads, optimize ads and to remarket ads to people who've already shown some interest or taken any kind of action on the website.

The Facebook Pixel works by placing and activating cookies to track users as they interact with the website the Pixel is on and the advertiser's Facebook ads. There used to be a few different types of pixels; the Facebook custom audience pixel and the Facebook conversion pixel, however in 2017, Facebook discontinued the conversion tracking pixel.

Simple Guide to Creating a Facebook Pixel

As explained earlier, the Facebook pixel is a code placed on your website to build an audience, report conversion, and receive insights about how visitors are using your website. Users can create up to a hundred pixels in their

Business Manager account on Facebook.

You'd probably want to build a Facebook pixel in Business Manager if:

- You have a Business Manager account on Facebook.
- Someone else looks after and manages your Facebook ads.
- The business has more than one primary service or product.
- The company has more than one website.
- Take advantage of pixel's measurement abilities, but you are not yet ready for creating ads.

Step by Step Guide to Creating a Facebook Pixel

Before you begin, ensure that you've access to a Business Manager account; if not, create one. And make sure that you are an admin of the account that you would like to use.

Read on to know how you can create a Facebook pixel in Business Manager:

Step #1: Head to the business settings in the Business Manager.

Step #2: Select your business.

Step #3: Click on 'Data Sources'.

Step #4: Select 'Pixels'.

Step #5: Click on the + Add button.

Step #6: Enter a name for the pixel.

Step #7: Enter your webpage URL (optional).

Step #8: Click on the Continue button.

Step #9: To install the pixel on your website, click the 'Set up the pixel now' button.

If you would like to stay on the Business Manager page, click 'Continue managing my business' option.

Once the Facebook pixel is set up, it will start working as soon as someone takes action on the website. For example, making a purchase or adding an item to the shopping basket are actions. The pixel receives these events or activities which can be viewed in Events Manager on the Facebook pixel page. From there, you will be able to view the actions that your customers take and will also get the option to reach them again through future Facebook ads (remarketing).

Why Set Up a Facebook Pixel?

The Facebook pixel offers significant information that can be used to target your ads better and create improved Facebook ads in the future. The tracking data provided by Facebook pixel helps you make sure that the ad is seen by people who will most likely take your desired action. Moreover, this allows businesses to improve their Facebook ad conversion rate and receive a higher return on investment.

Even if you are not using Facebook ads yet, you should install the Facebook pixel. It'll start collecting data immediately so that you're well equipped and do not have to start from scratch once you're ready to explore the world of Facebook ads.

Here are a few significant reasons to set up a Facebook

pixel.

1. Facebook Conversion Tracking

The Facebook pixel allows business managers to view how people interact with their website after watching their ads on Facebook. It even allows them to track customers across their devices and helps them to discover if customers tend to view their ads on mobile but later switch to a desktop before making the purchase or vice versa. This information can help owners to refine their ad strategy and also calculate their ROI.

2. Facebook Retargeting

Data from the Facebook retargeting pixel and dynamic ads help you show targeted ads to customers who've previously visited your website. Businesses can choose to be granular or specific here. For instance, ads related to the products that were earlier abandoned by a customer can again be shown to the exact people.

3. Lookalike Audiences

Facebook can use the targeting data to help build a lookalike audience of individuals with similar interests, likes, and demographics to individuals who are currently interacting with your website. This is a great way to expand the potential customer base.

4. Augment Facebook Ads for Conversion

Data from Facebook tracking pixel can be used to alleviate

your Facebook ads for particular conversion events on your site. Without a pixel, the only conversion you can augment for is link clicks. With Facebook pixel, you can optimize for leads that align closely with your business goals, like sign-ups and purchases.

5. Alleviate Facebook Ads for Value

As Facebook gathers data on who buys from your website and how much money they spend, it allows you to optimize your ad audience based on value; meaning that it'll automatically show ads to customers who are most likely to make high-value purchases.

Sharing and Editing Your Facebook Pixel

There may be a few scenarios in which you'd like to edit the name of your Pixel or even share it. Here's how:

Editing the Name of Your Facebook Pixel

To edit the name of your Facebook Pixel, go to the Pixels page in Business Manager and click on the Pixel you'd like to edit. From the upper menu, click on the pencil icon next to your Pixel to edit the name.

To share your Pixel, click on your Pixel on the Pixels page in Business Manager. Once you've done this, click on "Share" in the upper-right corner of the top menu. Next, enter the name of the individual that you'd like to share your Pixel with.

Easy peasy.

Troubleshooting Your Facebook Pixel

There will likely come a time in which your Pixel malfunctions and you receive a warning or error message indicating you need to troubleshoot your Facebook Pixel. You may find yourself at a loss and frustrated - I know I sure was when I first started.

On the diagnostics tab of your Facebook Pixels page (in Business Manager), you can see a list of issues that may be preventing your pixel from sending accurate data. In here, you'll also find information on how to resolve the issues and a list of affected URLs and parameters.

Facebook Pixel Helper

The Facebook Pixel Helper is a Google Chrome extension that you can install for free. This handy helper troubleshoots issues with your Pixel and can help improve performance.

Once this tool is installed, you'll be able to check whether your website (or any other website) has a Facebook Pixel installed, check for errors and understand the events that your Pixel is receiving.

Ads Manager

Ads Manager is where the magic happens. This is where you'll create those stunning and impactful ads to help you generate new leads and increase your revenue. To get to your Ads Manager account, open your Business Manager and click on the tab on the left-side menu titled Ads Manager.

If you're new to Facebook Ads and Ads Manager, it may look complicated, but trust me, it gets easier with knowledge and practice. Let's work on the knowledge portion of that and talk it through.

Three Levels of Ads Manager

There are three levels to Ads Manager, and they are: The Campaign level, the Ad Sets level and the Ads level.

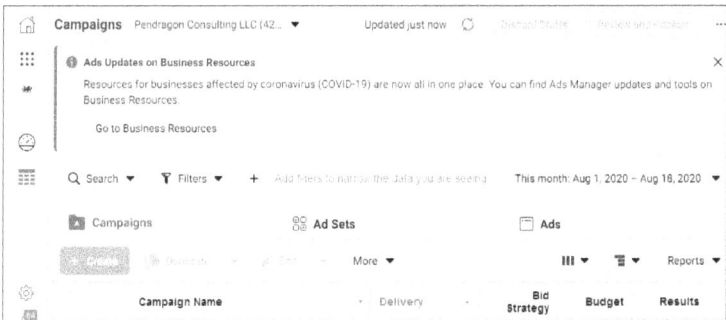

Figure-11

Campaign Level

The Campaign Level is where you would choose whether you're advertising in a special ad category, your objective (i.e. drive traffic, lead generation, conversions, etc.), name your campaign, as well as create A/B split tests and your campaign budget optimization.

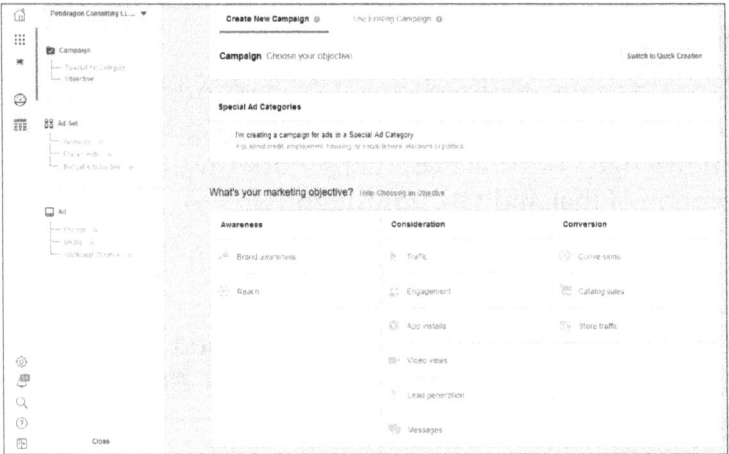

Figure-12

Ad Set Level

In the Ad Set Level, you'll be able to name the ad set, select which page you're advertising for (*if* you manage more than one Facebook Page), choose your audience, select where you'd like your ads shown (important if you're a financial advisor who cannot use Instagram!), set your budget and schedule, setup dayparting if you're going that route and choose either a daily or lifetime budget.

Ad Level

The Ad Level is where you can get creative. This is where you'll be building the ad itself with creatives, copy, links and your lead form if you're conducting lead generation.

Pro-Tip: Build your lead form in advance in the Leads Center of your Facebook Business Page for easy selection of forms when building your ad.

If you've opted in for A/B split testing, or are creating multiple ads, you'll have more than one section of Ad Level when setting your ads up. In Ads Manager, in the Ads tab, you'll see all of your ads with the various audiences or creatives populate there.

Ads Manager Features

If you're managing multiple accounts, you can toggle between them at the top. There are also a few other key features that may come in handy. For instance, if you've deleted an ad by mistake or just wanted to get some more information from it, you can go back through your deleted ads by clicking on Filter followed by Campaign Deliver and then Deleted.

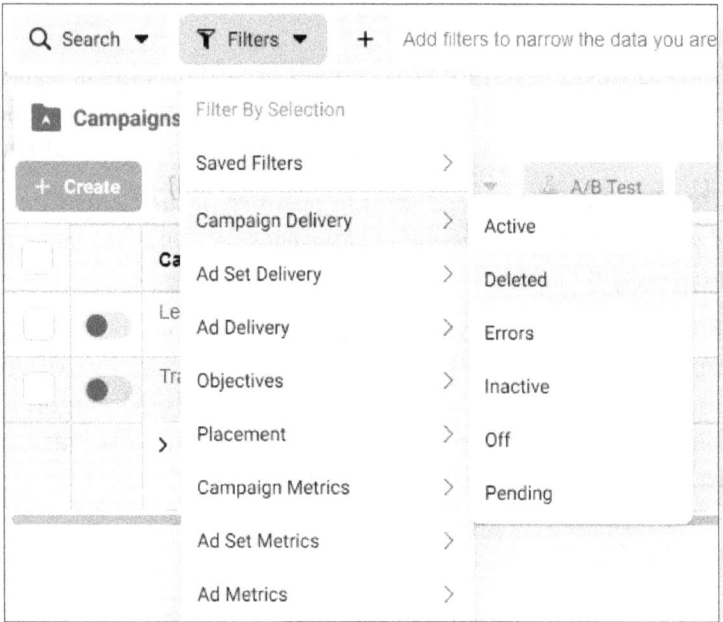

Figure-13

You cannot restart a deleted campaign; however, you can duplicate it and then run it as a new ad.

Facebook's Non-Discrimination Policy

Now we come to the point of contention. Facebook has come under fire these last few weeks (month, years…) for certain issues, such as moderating toxic content. In fact, beginning in June of 2020, big names began boycotting Facebook Advertising. As a result, Facebook has tightened up a few of its policies on hate speech, including instituting bans on advertisements that promote discrimination against people based on their race, ethnicity, sexual orientation, gender or immigration status. (Think special ad categories such as housing, employment and credit opportunities.)

In order to advertise on Facebook, you'll need to certify compliance with Facebook's Non-Discrimination Policy.

Here's the official Policy:

Non-Discrimination Policy

"Ads must not discriminate or encourage discrimination against people based on personal attributes such as race, ethnicity, color, national origin, religion, age, sex, sexual orientation, gender identity, family status, disability, medical or genetic condition.

Facebook prohibits advertisers from using our ads products to discriminate against people. This means that advertisers may not (1) use our audience selection tools to (a) wrongfully target specific groups of people for advertising (see Advertising Policy 7.1 on Targeting), or (b) wrongfully exclude specific groups of people from seeing their ads; or (2) include discriminatory content in their ads. Advertisers are also required to comply with applicable laws that prohibit discrimination (see Advertising Policy 4.2 on Illegal Products or Services). These include laws that prohibit discriminating against groups of people in connection with, for example, offers of housing, employment, and credit.

Any United States advertiser or advertiser targeting the United States that is running credit, housing or employment ads, must self-identify as a **Special Ad Category**, as it becomes available, and run such ads with approved targeting options."

You can read the policy on Facebook's website here:

https://www.facebook.com/policies/ads/prohibited_content/discriminatory_practices#

Certifying Compliance

At the onset of creating your Ads manager account, you'll have to certify compliance with the social platform's Non-Discrimination Policy. Here's what that will look like:

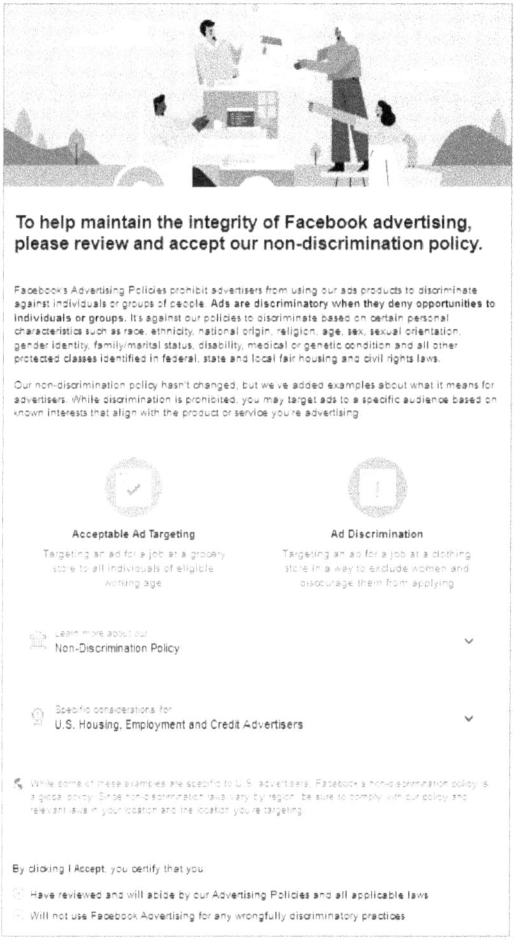

Figure-14

The Non-Discrimination Policy dropdown takes you to the policy which we've provided just before the image. Check out what is considered "acceptable" and "discrimination" for housing, employment and credit advisors:

Specific considerations for
U.S. Housing, Employment and Credit Advertisers

While we are asking all advertisers to review and accept our non-discrimination policy, it's especially important for advertisers running housing, employment or credit ads because of the history of discrimination in these categories.

Opportunities presented in these types of ads must be inclusive and extended to all groups of people, regardless of certain personal attributes like those listed above. Many locations have laws that specifically prohibit discrimination in these categories.

Acceptable Ad Targeting	Ad Discrimination
✓ **Housing Targeting** Targeting an ad for an apartment rental to people who live within a 15-mile radius of the location of the listing	✕ **Housing Discrimination** Targeting an ad for an apartment rental that excludes certain ZIP codes with the intent to deny it to people of a certain race or ethnicity
✓ **Employment Targeting** Targeting an ad for a job as a salesperson to people interested in sales and marketing	✕ **Employment Discrimination** Targeting an ad for a job as a salesperson in a way intended to exclude women
✓ **Credit Targeting** Targeting an ad for a credit card to all individuals of eligible age	✕ **Credit Discrimination** Targeting an ad for a credit card that attempts to exclude individuals of a specific national origin

Figure-15

Once you've certified compliance with their policy, you'll be able to begin setting up in Ads Manager.

Prohibited and Restricted Content

There are a number of things that go against Facebook's policies in terms of what you can and cannot advertise. Below, you'll find a list of prohibited and restricted topics for Facebook Advertising.

Prohibited Content

- Anything that violates community standards
- Illegal products or services
- Discriminatory Practices* (see next chapter on non-discrimination)
- Tobacco and related products
- Drugs and drug-related products
- Unsafe supplements
- Weapons, ammunition or explosives
- Adult products or services
- Adult content
- Third-Part infringement
- Sensational content
- Personal attributes
- Misinformation
- Controversial content
- Non-functional landing page
- Cheating and deceitful practices
- Grammar and profanity
- Nonexistent functionality
- Personal health
- Payday loans, paycheck advances and bail bonds
- Multilevel marketing
- Penny auctions
- Misleading claims

- Low quality or disruptive content
- Spyware or malware
- Automatic animation
- Unacceptable business practices
- Circumventing systems
- Prohibited financial products and services
- Sale of body parts

Restricted Content

- Alcohol
- Dating
- Real money gambling
- State lotteries
- Online pharmacies
- Promotion of over the counter drugs
- Subscription services
- Financial and insurance products and services
- Branded content
- Ads about social issues, elections or politics
- Disclaimers for ads about social issues, elections or politics
- Cryptocurrency products and services
- Drug and alcohol addiction treatment
- Cosmetic procedures and weight loss

Special Ad Categories

We talked about Facebook's policy on restricted and prohibited topics for advertisements (refer back to the chapter on Policies). Here's where it can get tricky…

Facebook has "Special Ad Categories" for hot button issues - such as housing, employment, credit, social issues, elections and politics.

In August of 2019, Facebook announces that it would now require all U.S.-based advertisers of housing, credit and employment to select the "special ad category" option in Facebook Ads Manager when creating new ads focused on one of those areas. As a way of preventing discrimination, Facebook has restricted certain targeting options. Advertisers in the special ads categories are no longer able to target based on age, gender, zip code, multicultural affinity or any other protected characteristics. In addition to restricting targeting of certain demographics, they have also prohibited advertisers from using Facebook's Lookalike Audience ad feature.

The categories of social issues, elections, and politics have only recently come about in June of 2020. In addition to adding those issues as a special ad category, Facebook will be giving its users the ability to turn off posts regarding social issues, elections and politics from candidates, Super PACs or other organizations that have the "paid for by" political disclaimer on them.

Facebook came under fire this summer for a number of reasons. The 2020 election, COVID-19 misinformation and even a large advertising boycott. Love it or hate it, you can't deny the social media giant still has some progress to make - and they're not the only platform either.

So, what does this mean for you as an advertiser? It means that if you're advertising for something in a special ad category, you have a few extra hoops to jump through.

Social Issues, Elections and Politics

What constitutes an ad on these topics?

Facebook states that the following constitute an ad that would fall under this category:

- *"Made by, on behalf of, or about a candidate for public office, a political figure, a political party or advocates for the outcome of an election to public office; or*
- *About any election, referendum, or ballot initiative, including "go out and vote" or election campaigns; or*
- *About social issues in any place where the ad is being placed; or*
- *Regulated as political advertising."*

This information is an excerpt from Facebook's Business Help Center. More information is available here: https://www. facebook.com/business/help/167836590566506

Verification and Authorization

If you are trying to advertise on a political, election or social issues, you *must be authorized by Facebook before* you can run any ads on that category. Only individuals from certain countries are eligible to apply. To see the full list of countries, please visit:

https://www.facebook.com/business/
208949576550051

By August 5th, advertisers in selected countries will be required to get authorized and set disclaimers to run electoral or political ads.

Due to new disclaimer requirements in Brazil to run electoral and political ads all existing disclaimers will need to be replaced by August 5th.

Given the evolving COVID-19 situation, we have fewer people and resources available to process new authorizations for ads about social issues, elections or politics. In certain cases, our review times to review ID documents has exceeded 48 hours. Our teams are actively working to review your documents in a timely manner. Please continue to visit www.facebook.com/id to check status. If it's been 30 days or more since you submitted your ID and you haven't received a notification that it's been rejected or approved, try submitting your ID again. We apologize for any inconvenience.

Figure-16

In order to be authorized to run ads in this category, you'll need:

- To be the page admin
- Have two-factor authentication enabled
- Have unexpired materials and information available:
  - U.S. Passport, driver's license or ID card
  - A U.S.-based residential mailing address

Facebook uses this information to confirm your identity as well as to prevent risks of impersonation and identity theft, keeping you and the Facebook community "safe."

If after your verification and authorization is completed and approved you turn off your two-factor authentication, your disclaimers and ads will be disabled.

Housing

If you're a real estate agent/agency, this section is for you. Any property listings, whether for sale or for rent, homeowners insurance, mortgage insurance, mortgage loans, housing repairs and home equity or appraisals, must select this special ad category when running advertisements AND must comply with Facebook's Advertising Policies.

One of the main objectives of, really all of the special ad categories, is to prevent discrimination. Before this, advertisers were allowed to exclude certain individuals from being able to see their ads (in this case, property listings, etc.).

Audience Selection Options
We encourage you to broaden and not restrict your audience. To help you comply with our Advertising Policies, some audience selection options are unavailable or limited when running ads in this special category.

Age
Options are fixed to include ages 18 through 65+ and can't be changed.

Gender
Options are fixed to include all genders and can't be changed.

Detailed Targeting
Some detailed targeting options, which may include demographics, behaviors or interests, are unavailable. Excluding any detailed targeting selections is unavailable.

Location
ZIP code selection is unavailable. Location selection must include all areas within a 15-mile radius of any selected city, address or dropped pin.

Lookalike Audiences
Lookalike audiences are unavailable. To reach new people, you can create a Special Ad Audience that includes people with online behavior similar to your most valuable customers.

Custom Audiences
When using a Custom Audience, be sure that your audience selections do not discriminate against people based on certain personal characteristics.

Saved Audiences
Using previously saved audiences or saving a new audience is unavailable.

Figure-17

Employment

It does not matter what industry you're in, if you're advertising for an employment position within your company, you must select the special ad category and comply with Facebook's Advertising Policies. This is another category that has previously been abused, with discrimination running rampant. Employment opportunities include, but are not limited to:

- Part-time
- Full-time
- Internships
- Professional certification programs

Facebook has restricted the options for targeting certain demographics in order to enforce non-discrimination.

Credit

Any ads that either promote or directly link to a credit opportunity or related service falls under Facebook's special ad category and should be selected when creating your advertisement. Facebook considers the following to be credit-related advertisements:

- Credit card offers
- Auto loans
- Personal loans
- Business loans
- Mortgage loans
- Long-term financing

If your company is offering any of these services, you must select this special ad category and comply with their Advertising policies. Similar to housing and employment, credit ads are also restricted from excluding or targeting certain demographics in their ads.

Transparency

In order to be more transparent, Facebook created the Ads Library. You're able to view a report in which will show you things like who is spending how much on the social issues, political and election special ad category.

To view the transparency report, please visit:

https://www.facebook.com/ads/library/report

Types of Facebook Ads

You can use a variety of different types of Facebook ads and get your message across to the right set of eyes.

Here are the types you can choose from:

1. Image

You see these ads on your News Feed with the word *sponsored* appearing right below the name of the business or brand. These feature an image – quite obvious – and a catchy tagline or caption to go with it. It is usually linked to the business' website or e-Commerce shop or a landing page.

This is the simplest form of Facebook ads and can be created with only a few clicks.

2. Video

Like the image ad – but with a video or GIF, video ads can appear on News Feed or in Facebook Stories. They can also appear as in-stream ads – i.e. ads that you see in long videos (YouTube videos often has in-stream ads).

The goal here is to engage the audience and make use of the fact that video posts on Facebook generate 6.12% engagement compared to the 3.5% rate of average engagement.

3. Carousel

Just like the amusement park ride, Facebook carousel ads

feature multiple images or videos in a slide-show type of format. Each image or video can give a little more insight into your product or service. These can also be used to create an eye-catching panorama.

You can also create slide-show ads using the stock images available on Facebook Ads.

4. Instant Experience

The true way of bringing Facebook Ads to life!

Previously called Canvas, Instant Experiences are full-screen ads that highlight your brand in various formats, whether its video, image, carousel, collection, etc. You can further embed links and text buttons to divert the audience onto other sources.

5. Collection

Collection ads are paid ads that you can use to "create a collection" and showcase five or fewer products or services. This is a great option for clothing brands and such that release new products as a part of a collection, by adding buttons and linking the ad to your website to make online shopping easier.

6. Lead Ads

Leads ads on Facebook are specially designed for mobile devices. As the name suggests, the purpose here is to gain a prospect's information and qualify them as a lead. The ad shows up as an "instant form" that the viewer can fill out without spending too much time on it. It's a great tool for B2B sales funnels. While you can opt to use some standard questions on the lead form, you also can create a custom lead form as well.

While these sum up the basic types of Facebook ads, there are others such as Facebook Messenger ads where you can further access 1.3 billion people.

Other types or rather, sub-types of ads include dynamic ads, which let you target specific audiences with particular products; and augmented ads that include filters and animations that allow audiences to interact with the ad.

Jessica Ainsworth

Understanding the Ad Budget

We are sure that everyone is well aware of how beneficial Facebook ads can prove to be for businesses and marketers alike, but have you ever wondered about the price that needs to be paid for all the good?

That indeed is a tricky question!

But the simplest answer is, it will never cost you more than what you have to spend. For example, if you've set a budget of $10 per day, Facebook Ads will never charge you more than $10 a day. Nevertheless, numerous factors will affect the success you will see for your investment and how far the budget will stretch.

Maybe a healthier approach with Facebook Ads would be to consider how you can make your budget convey the best results for your brand. And that is precisely where we would love to help you today.

But first, let's understand the different budget options in Facebook ads. To realize and comprehend how to make a budget work for you.

Ready to read on?

What is an Ad Budget?

A budget is the amount of money that a person is willing to spend to show people their ads. It is also an excellent tool for cost control as it helps to control the overall expend for an ad set or campaign.

An ad budget refers to a budget being applied to an ad

set as a whole and hence, is not determined per ad. The amount of money you spend on an ad campaign depends significantly on how much funds you allocate to each ad set.

Budgets can be set either at the ad set or campaign level. Additionally, there are two available budget options in Facebook ads: daily and lifetime.

What is a Daily Budget?

A daily ad budget is an average amount you are willing to devote to an ad campaign or set each day. Meaning that Facebook will try to get you results around your daily budget's worth every day. Your budget will not be disbursed evenly across the life of your ad campaign, as certain instances will be more superior for connecting with your target audience than others.

At such times, around 25 percent over your daily budget may be consumed. For instance, if your daily budget is $10, Facebook may spend up to $12.50 on a given day. This allows Facebook to spend your budget and deliver the ads as efficiently as possible.

What is a Lifetime Budget?

A lifetime budget is a total sum that you are willing to pay over the entire run of your campaign or ad set. You will not be charged for more than your lifetime budget for your campaign or ad set's results.

If you are using standard delivery, Facebook endeavors to spend your budget evenly over the ad set's life. However, there are no guarantees that the same quantity will be exhausted each day as Facebook might be able to get you superior results on certain days.

For instance, if you have a $100 lifetime budget for an ad set that will be running for four days, $15 may be spent on the first two days. If, on the third day, considerable results are available, then Facebook might pay $50. Similarly, if there aren't many good opportunities on the fourth day, only $10 may be spent.

Daily Budget vs. Lifetime Budget

Now that you've understood what daily and lifetime budgets are, here is a brief review of the key times you would want to choose one of these budget options in Facebook ads over the other.

Choose lifetime budgets when:

- It would be best if you run your ads on a schedule.
- Your ad campaign has a pre-determined end date and a set budget.

Choose daily budgets when:

- You want to amplify strong performance.
- You want your campaign to remain evergreen.
- There's a need to change the ad budget regularly.

There is no wrong or right answer when it comes to picking a winner between daily budget vs. lifetime budget, but there are considerations to keep in mind. Depending on the kind of ad set or campaign you are running, you might have to make a hard choice, or if you're lucky, there may be a perfect option available. Thus, study your ad set or campaign and determine which option will be most lucrative for you.

How to Set Up an Ad Budget?

Let's look at a brief overview of how to set up an ad budget on Facebook:

1. Go to Ads Manager and select 'budget and schedule'.
2. Choose either a lifetime or daily budget from the drop-down list.
3. If you select a daily budget, specify the amount you are willing to pay on an ad set every day.
4. If you choose the lifetime budget, determine the total sum you are ready to pay over the ad set's complete runtime.
5. The next step is to set the schedule. You have the option to begin running your ad starting today or at some other future date.
6. In case of a future date, set a start and an end date for the schedule.
7. You also have the option to determine the time you want the ad set to run and end.
8. Now you'll see the maximum budget amount allotted and the total number of days determined for the ad set.
9. In case you choose a lifetime budget, you will have more options to refine the ad set schedule.
10. Once you are done, click on continue and specify which ads you want your budget to be spent on.

Facebook Ad Auction

Facebook ads are not rocket science, but you must understand how the system operates before you start running your ads. For each ad impression, the Facebook ad auction system chooses the ads with the most potential to run on the ad performance and ads' maximum bids.

If you want to use Facebook ads effectively, you must develop a deep understanding of how the Facebook ad auction works. There are countless people out there using Facebook ads, but most probably would fail to explain what this is or how it works.

Truth be told, it is an incredibly crucial concept, and if you're not aware of how to cater to the auction, then you, my friend, are playing at a disadvantage.

This chapter has been created in order to cover specifically how the Facebook ad auction works and how you can tailor your ads to receive optimal results.

What is Facebook Ad Auction?

The majority of ad campaigns or ad sets that you run or see on Facebook are using this auction system. Every time an individual is exposed to an ad on the Facebook platform, an ad auction takes place. But unlike other auction systems, on Facebook's ad auction system, you cannot win with just the highest bid.

Facebook continuously endeavors to find the best ad-user fit because Facebook realizes that it needs to keep both parties happy. For this purpose, it ensures that relevant ads are shown to the right users while keeping advertisement costs low for advertisers.

Why is it Vital to Know How the Auction Works?

The results generated by Facebook ads are greatly affected by the ad bidding and auction system. Therefore, if you are not set up and well prepared for success with the auction, two possible things can happen:

1. You'll have to pay a lot of money for meaningful ad results, which could make the entire campaign unprofitable. This outcome is almost guaranteed if you fail to make the right bids.
2. The second thing that could occur is that your ads might never get delivered in the first. Failing to meet the bidding criteria will ultimately make you lose the chance of any profit.

How Does the Facebook Ad Auction Work?

The Facebook ad auction system works by computing the highest total value. An algorithm that comprises three essential parts is used in this process. The three key components of total value are:

1. Bid
2. Estimated action rates
3. Ad Quality

Continue reading to learn more about each.

Bid

The most evident and significant aspect of the system is the bid marketers pay for an ad. When you set up an ad campaign, you inform Facebook about how much money you're willing to pay for a desired outcome or conversion. This information is shared on Facebook through a few bidding strategies, such as:

- Bid cap – to be able to control your bid in every auction; the best option if you're wanting to control costs while reaching as many people as possible.
- Highest value or lowest cost– receive the most purchase value or volume of results for your budget.
- Target cost - receive a consistent cost per result.
- Cost cap – Control costs while receiving the most volume results for your budget.

Bids are placed at the ad set level so you can easily play around within campaigns. However, bidding is just one element of the Facebook ad auction system.

Ultimately, this number is the amount that you are willing to pay for the desired outcome (i.e. a lead, a conversion, etc.)

Estimated Action Rates

Facebook has an enormous pool of data. This myriad of data is used to determine the likelihood of someone engaging with your ad or figuring out the possibility of someone performing your desired action. To do so, Facebook studies the past search history of the targeted user, and from this, it determines whether they are a suitable candidate for your ad or not. Facebook does this because it wants to create value for both users. By showing useful and relevant ads to viewers and offering low costs to advertisers.

Just ensure that you are not deliberately asking people to engage with or post on your ad. Moreover, avoid click-baiting as well because both of these tactics will land you in a low ad quality score.

Ad Quality

The final aspect of the Facebook ad auction system is the quality of an ad. Several factors are used to determine the quality of an ad, such as:

Negative Feedback: One of the factors affecting ad quality is the negative feedback that users give after seeing an ad. A typical example of negative feedback on Facebook is when people click on 'hide ads' they do not wish to see. Negative feedback on one ad can significantly increase the cost across all ads and, perhaps worse, can adversely affect your account's reputation.

Positive Feedback: On the flip side, positive feedback can lead to engagement generation and a lot of shares. Ultimately, enriching the quality of your ad. Positive feedback is essentially a free advertisement.

Other factors that Facebook looks at while determining ad quality are *landing pages* and *content*.

Low-quality content is defined as:

- Engagement bait
- Sensationalism
- Withholding integral information in the copy

A low-quality landing page is described as any webpage that has:

- No original content
- High bounce rate
- Many pop-up ads
- Unexpected website experience

Facebook will notify you with a warning message or penalty in case you have a low-quality ad score. Therefore, avoid doing anything that may result in poor user experience.

Now that you're well informed about how the Facebook ad auction works, you will be better equipped and prepared while setting up your ads. Ensure you have a high-quality ad score and implement a solid bidding strategy. By following these instructions, you can trust Facebook to show your ads to the right audience, at the right price.

Jessica Ainsworth

Building a Facebook Ad

Step Zero – Strategy Development

Before you begin creating a campaign, have a quick brainstorming session to figure out what your strategy entails. There are too many options available on Facebook Ads to be confused and distracted by.

Begin by answering simple questions. For example, what is the product or service you want to advertise? Who is the target audience? Is it a cold audience or warm? Does the product/service solve their problem? What is their pain point? Is the campaign toward lead generation, brand awareness, traffic diversion, or sales?

These will give you a rough blueprint of where you are and where you want to be at the end.

Step 1 – Choosing the Objective of the Campaign

With a strategy in place, you can dive into creating a campaign. Once your Facebook Business Page is created, go to the Ad Manager and click on **Campaigns**. If this is your first time creating any sort of ad, the page will say *No Results Found*.

Click on the **Create Ad** button to begin (as shown through red arrows).

Figure-18

The ad manager will then ask you to choose an objective for the campaign. As shown in the picture below, there are three main categories and a total of eleven objectives to choose from.

1. Brand awareness
2. Reach
3. Traffic
4. Engagement
5. App Installation
6. Video views
7. Lead generation
8. Message
9. Conversions
10. Catalog sales
11. Store traffic

Most of these objectives are pretty self-explanatory as to what goal they aim to achieve. Choose one that aligns with the goal you set for the campaign in Step Zero. However, if you get stuck, there's a little information icon on each tab that you can hover over. That will bring up a dialog box providing a basic description. By clicking on "Learn More", it will open a column on the right side of the page providing a bit more insight into just what you can accomplish with that objective.

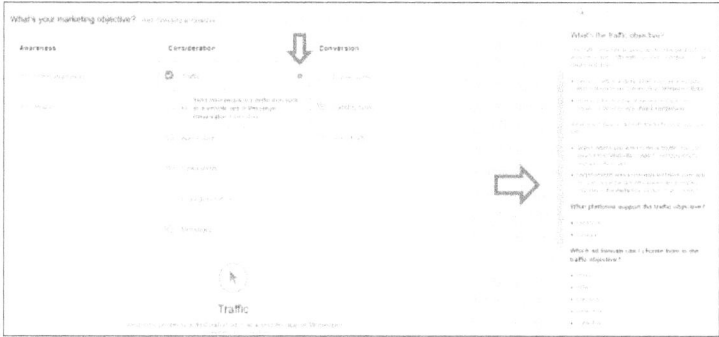

Figure-19

One important point to note here is that paid advertisements for objectives will vary. For instance, if your campaign is directed at driving conversions, you will be paying cost-per-action. On the other hand, traffic engaging ads involve costs per impressions.

Step 2 – Choosing the Name & Creating an Ad Account

After you've chosen your objective, the page, as shown in the picture below will show up. As you can see, the prompt requires you to name the campaign.

This is also where you can choose to optimize your budget, which is recommended if you're creating multiple ad sets; and run an AB split test to see how you can maximize the ad's effectiveness. *Depending on the objective you choose, not all budget options will be available.*

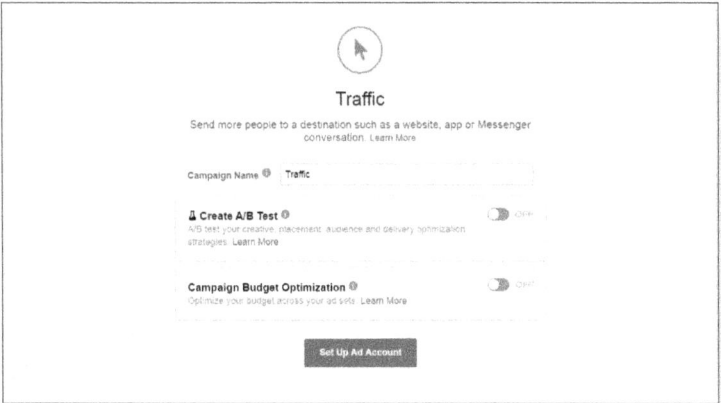

Figure-20

The next step is clicking on the "Set up Ad Account" button, which will then ask you for information such as your preferred location, time zone, currency, etc.

Step 3 – Selecting a Target Audience

The step right after you *Set up an Ad Account* will be different depending on the objective you choose. In this example, we chose Traffic as our objective. The next prompts for this option are shown in the image below:

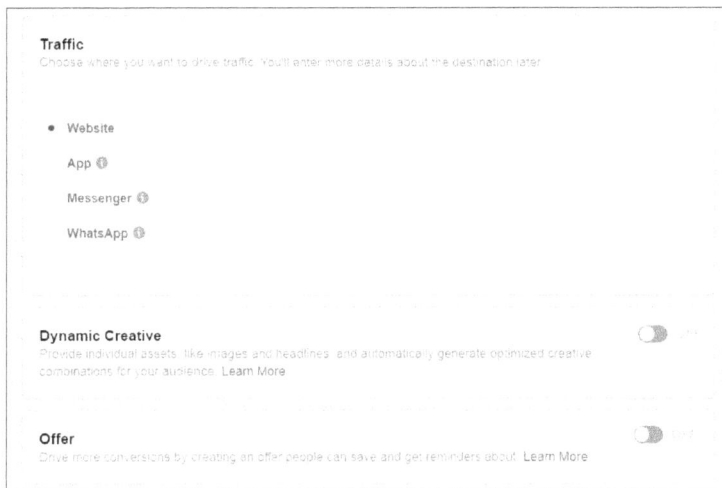

Traffic
Choose where you want to drive traffic. You'll enter more details about the destination later.

• Website

App ⓘ

Messenger ⓘ

WhatsApp ⓘ

Dynamic Creative
Provide individual assets, like images and headlines, and automatically generate optimized creative combinations for your audience. Learn More

Offer
Drive more conversions by creating an offer people can save and get reminders about. Learn More

Figure-21

The main step here is creating your target audience for the campaign. You can create a new audience or use a previously saved audience. The next step will be targeting your audience. The four main selections here are:

• Choosing the location and selecting whether you want to target people living or recently living, just living, just traveling or recently in this particular location
• Choosing the age range of your audience
• Choosing the gender identity of your audience
• Choosing the language

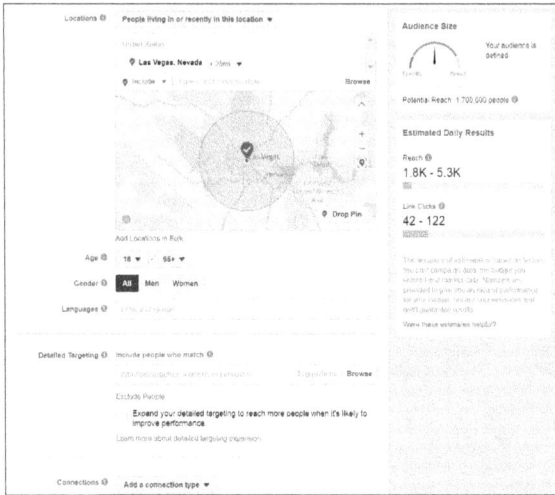

Figure-22

The Detailed Targeting prompt lets you include or exclude certain audiences. You can make your selections based on the audience's behavior. Facebook allows you to get very specific. Make use of detailed targeting to maximize your outreach to the **right** audience for a particular campaign.

You can also define your connection type. For example, you can set this prompt to:

- People who like your page
- Friends of people who like your page
- Exclude people who like your page

There are other and more advanced combinations you can create to further narrow down your target audience. You can even set up multiple audiences (one at a time). This is especially helpful if you're looking to target people who have been captured in your Facebook Pixel AND a defined target audience on Facebook or other combinations.

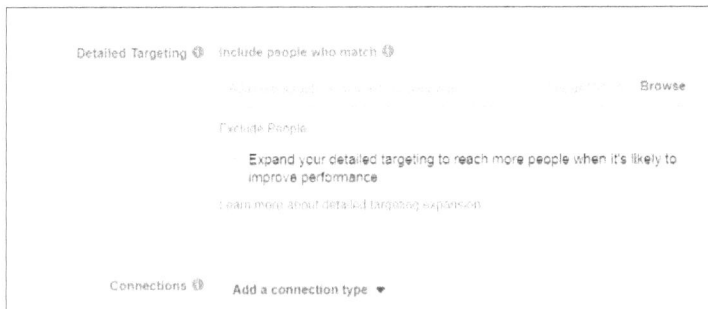

Figure-23

Step 4 – Choosing Ad Placements

In this step, you're essentially defining *where* your targeted audience will see the ads. You can go with the recommended option as it automatically allocates your budget across various Facebook platforms for maximum reach. For businesses that don't want to target Instagram, this is where you'll need to uncheck the box to ensure your ads aren't shown there. This is especially important for those in the financial sector who are not authorized to advertise on Instagram.

In **Manual Placements**, you get to decide the following:

- Device types (mobile or desktop or all)
- Platforms
  - Instagram
  - Facebook
  - Messenger
  - Audience Network
- Placements
  - Messenger

- News Feed
- Apps
- Stories
- More

These decisions will help narrow down and streamline your reach.

In **Automatic Placements**, where your ad will be shown and how your budget will be allocated will be determined by Facebook.

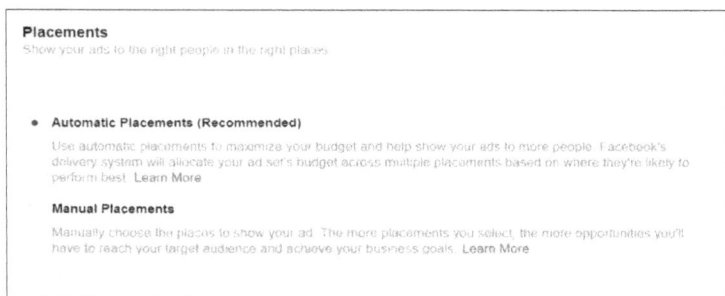

Placements
Show your ads to the right people at the right places

- **Automatic Placements (Recommended)**
  Use automatic placements to maximize your budget and help show your ads to more people. Facebook's delivery system will allocate your ad set's budget across multiple placements based on where they're likely to perform best. Learn More

  Manual Placements

  Manually choose the places to show your ad. The more placements you select, the more opportunities you'll have to reach your target audience and achieve your business goals. Learn More

Figure-24

Step 5 – The Budget!

This is where difficult decisions are made. No, you don't have to dedicate thousands of dollars to your Facebook campaign. You can control your ad spend and choose either a daily or lifetime budget. Additional bids allow you to cap the amount you want to spend on each action.

As for scheduling, you can choose to run your ad continuously or set a start and end date – this will help you save costs. *The caveat here is that not all options will be available depending on the objective you've chosen.*

If you click on the **Advanced Options** button, you can

configure budget send details such as:

- When you get charged
- Ad scheduling
- Delivery types

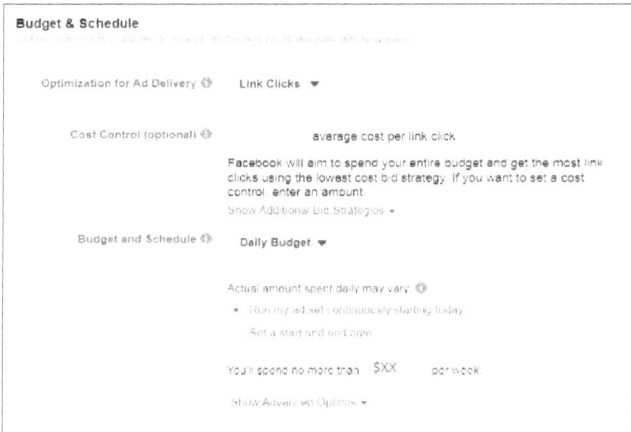

Figure-25

Step 6 – Ad Format Selection

Once you click **Continue,** you'll be directed to the page where you can create your ad. The first thing you will need to choose is the Ad Format. For *Traffic Ads*, the available options are depicted in the image below. You also get an option to add an Instant Experience (as explained before).

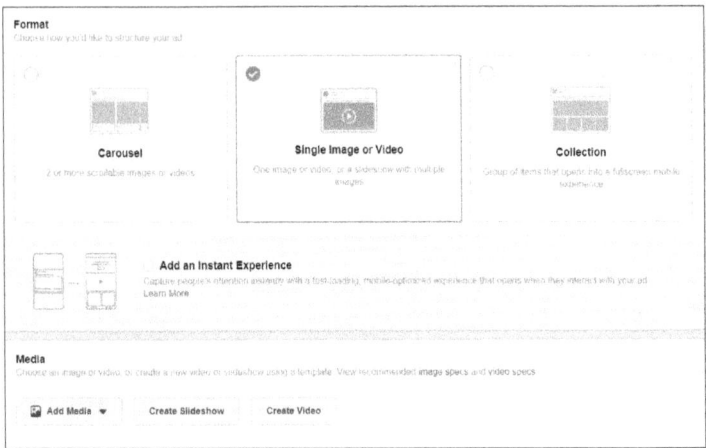

Figure-26

Depending on the Ad format you choose, you will have to fill out details pertaining to the ad. This involves adding the media (images or video), links, captions or ad copy, CTA (call to action), URL descriptions, destinations, etc. These details are essential for effectively disseminating the ad. You can check ad specs for each type of Facebook ad by clicking on the "i" or information tab next to each field.

If you're choosing to create an ad with an image, there are some best practices to be mindful of. Facebook has determined that images that have over 20% text do not perform as well. So, try to keep the amount of text on the image minimal. If you're unsure whether your image has too much text, you can use their tool to check the image. If your image isn't optimized, your ad may either be rejected, OR it may limit the number of people your ad will be shown to. While there are some exceptions, they are minimal. For instance, a picture of a book cover with wording on it may be exempt from the rule. You can learn more about best practices for your image by going to Facebook for Business "Business Help Center."

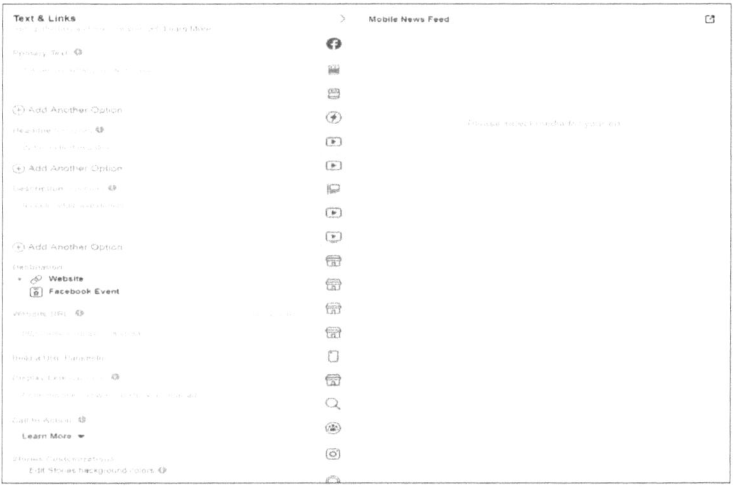

Figure-27

Step 7 – Monitor

With the ad now created and sent out into the digital landscape, all that's left is monitoring it. You can choose tracking metrics and set them up individually for each campaign you create. One example of a tracking metric would the Facebook Pixel, which we'll get into a bit later on.

If you're running multiple campaigns at the same time, Facebook Ad Manager lets you keep a check on the delivery, CPC, frequency, relevance score, impressions, reach, results, budget spent, etc.

These metrics are critical for measuring whether the ad is helping your ROI or not. You can use the insights to make changes to the campaigns to improve its performance.

Tracking

Conversion Tracking ⓘ

Facebook Pixel ⓘ   Set Up

App Events ⓘ   Set Up

Offline Events ⓘ   Set Up

URL Parameters (optional) ⓘ

    key1=value1&key2=value2

Build a URL Parameter

Figure-28

How to Share Facebook Ads

There may be some occasions in which you need to share an advertisement you've created in Facebook Ads Manager with someone. For instance, if your supervisor needs to approve the ad before you turn it live.

So, once you've finished setting up your advertisement, here's what you need to do:

In ads manager, you'll see three tabs: Campaigns, Ad Sets and Ads. Click on the tab called Ads.

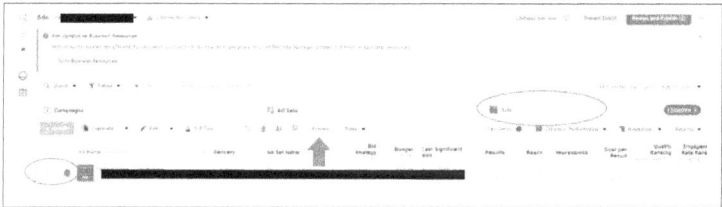

Figure-29

Once you've clicked on the "Ads" tab, go ahead and select the ad you'd like to share and then click on "Preview."

In the preview window that pops up, click on the button next to "Ad Preview," and you'll see several options that allow you to either send a share link, a notification on Facebook or Instagram.

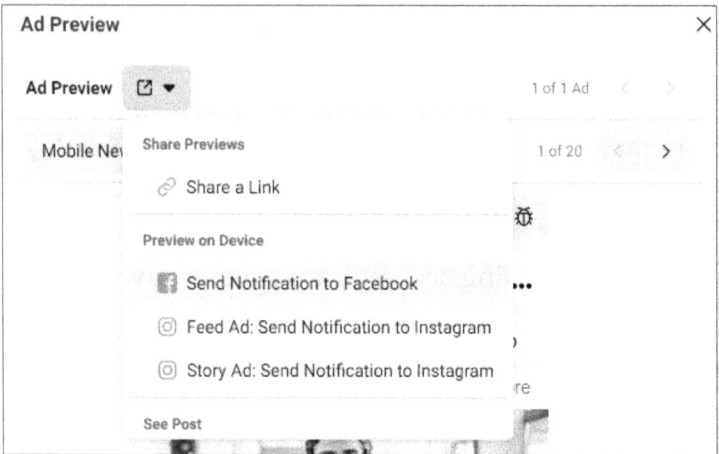

Figure-30

Once you've shared the advertisement and they've clicked to view the shared ad, it will show up in their Facebook Newsfeed, so they may need to scroll down a post or two for it to populate. Easy peasy, right?!

Creating Lead Forms

Lead Forms

If you've chosen lead generation as your objective, you have two ways of creating forms. The first is through the ad itself. This method is optimal if you're just looking to capture name, email, phone number, etc. - just the basics. While you'll have the ability to create your questions, they are short answer form, and you cannot create multiple-choice questions.

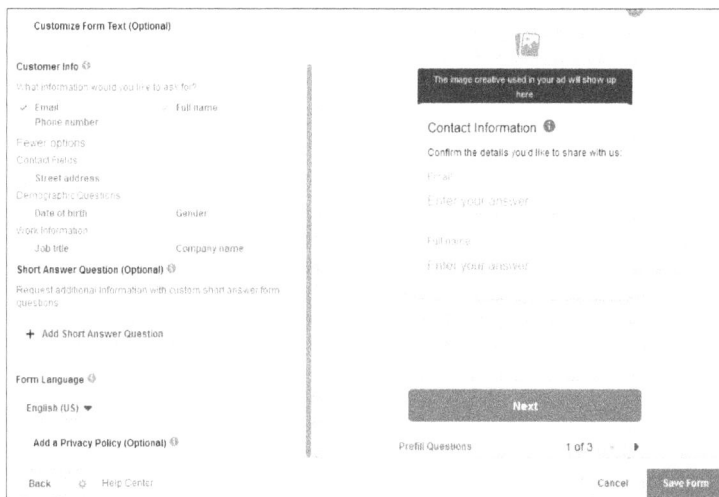

Figure-31

The other option would be to create your form through your actual Facebook Business page instead of through Business Manager. Once you've created your form, you'll need to come back into the Ads Manager to create the actual advertisement, but you'll have the option of using the form you just created.

On your Facebook page, click on "Publishing Tools." You may need to click "More" to find the publishing tools option once you have that open, select "Forms Library" from the right-side menu. Next, you'll want to click "create" to begin making your custom form.

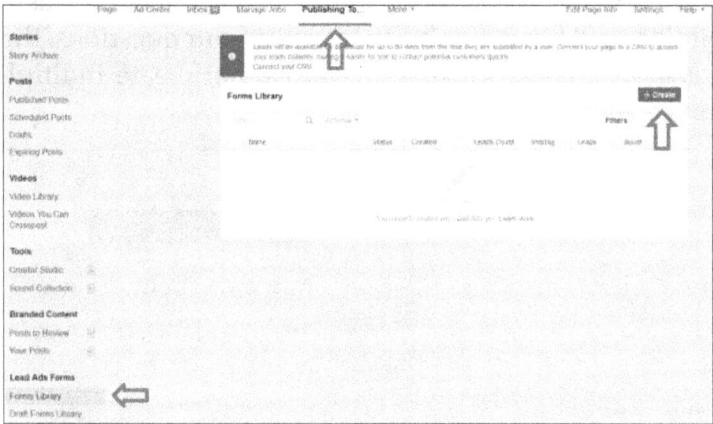

Figure-32

There will be some prompts you'll have to sort through after creating the new ad. You'll need to decide if you'd like more volume, which means an easier form to fill out for users OR if you'd like higher intent, meaning you have the option to add a review step to allow them to confirm their information. Once you've finished filling out the various sections, save your form before clicking "finish".

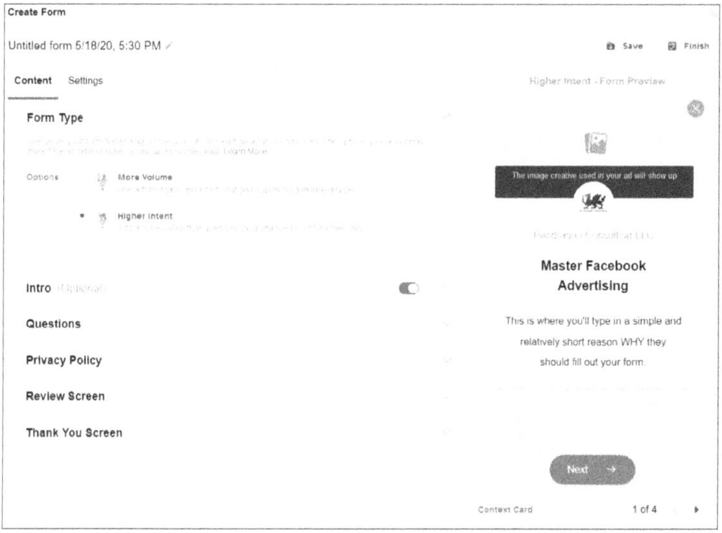

Figure-33

Now that you've created your custom form head back over into Ad Manager and set up your campaign as we've discussed through this book. When prompted, select the name of the lead form you just created.

After your advertisement has run its course, you may have returned some leads. To view them, under the publishing tool on your Facebook page, click on "forms library" once again. The various forms (if you created more than one) will have populated in there and will tell you whether there were any leads. You'll then have the option to download those leads into an XLS or CSV file. Alternatively, you can connect a CRM platform to have your leads sent through.

Jessica Ainsworth

Underperforming Ads

We've all been there… underperforming ads happen. Here are some ways you can improve your ads if you're faced with this dilemma:

Low Click-Through Rates

A Click-Through Rate (CTR) is the ratio of users who click on and/or engage with your content - in this case, your ad. If your CTR is low, you may need to adjust your ad as this could mean that your ad does not resonate well with your audience. Or you may need to change up your audience.

Low Impressions

The impressions indicate the number of times that your ad has been seen. The number of impressions is counted each and every time your ad is shown, even if someone has seen the ad two or three times. If you find that your ad is producing low impressions, this is a sign that your bid may be too low, and you're being outbid by your competitors. This means that your ad will be shown less, meaning fewer people see it and fewer impressions. The easy fix to this is simply to increase your bid.

Low Relevance Score

A relevance score is Facebook's measurement that shows the quality and engagement level of your advertisements. This is what sets your Cost Per Click (CPC) and how frequently your ad will be shown. A low relevance score means that you may need to change up your creatives to avoid giving your audience ad fatigue.

Low Reach

Reach is the number of unique people who saw your advertisement. A low reach means that not many people are seeing your ads. Your reach can be affected by your bid, budget and audience targeting. Consider increasing your bid if you have a large audience with low reach, as this could be a case of your competitors outbidding you.

High Cost Per Impressions

Cost Per Impressions (CPM) is a metric used to help you determine the cost-effectiveness of your ad campaign. This can also help you determine whether your ad is relevant to your audience. A high CPM is indicative that your ad has been deemed irrelevant to your audience by the Facebook powers that be. Well, your audience is ultimately the one who decides whether your ad is relevant. High CPM rates mean that you're paying more, and fewer people are seeing your ads. To improve this rate, you'll want to consider adjusting your target audience.

High Cost Per Click

The Cost Per Click (CPC) shows you how much each link click in your advertisement costs you. This metric is calculated by dividing the total amount spent by the number of link clicks. If you notice that you have a high CPC, you may want to pause your ad or even consider changing it. A high CPC usually means a lower ROI, and at that point, you have to ask if the hit to your budget is worth it if you're not getting enough in return.

Disapproved Ads

You can bet that at least once you'll experience Facebook rejecting your ads. It happens All. The. Time. Your ads are reviewed by both AI and by humans, so there's always the chance of a false disapproval, but more often than not, disapproval means that there's something wrong with your ad (i.e. something is typically not in compliance with Facebook's community standards or policies).

There are two options (a third if you're spending big bucks, like larger agencies) to get your ad approved. The first is to review both Facebook's policies and then go through to ensure that your ad is in compliance. If it isn't, you can edit the ad and resubmit it for approval.

If your ad has been disapproved and you believe that this was in error, you can appeal the disapproval. You will receive both an email notification of your disapproval, and there will also be a notification on your dashboard. It will also tell you a general reason for *why* your ad was disapproved. Again, if you think that the disapproval was in error, you are able to appeal the decision. You're able to appeal the decision by clicking on "appeal."

If you've looked over Facebook's policies for advertising, you'd have noticed that something as simple as grammar can get your ad rejected.

In addition to listing Facebook's ad policies in this book, you'll find the most current and up to date information on their website at:

https://www.facebook.com/policies/ads

Creating an Audience in Facebook Ads

Getting to know who your target customers or audience are is a critical step for an effective Facebook ads campaign. Several pieces of research show that Facebook has over one billion active users daily; hence it is absolutely vital that you target only those people who may potentially hold interest in your product or service. Expending marketing endeavors on people who are not likely to convert, is nothing but a waste of your resources.

Fortunately, Facebook provides a wide range of targeting opportunities that can assist you in finding the right niche for your ad campaign. In this step-by-step guide, you will learn everything about how to create an audience in Facebook ads.

Remember that successful advertising is not about getting cheap clicks; it's about attracting and retaining customers. Your cost per click *could be* as low as $0.3, but if your conversion rate is zero, then you're not just wasting your money but also your efforts. Hence, pick the audience who will meaningfully view your ads and keep testing your marketing endeavors by trying diverse targeting options and eventually find your sweet spot.

How to Create an Audience on Facebook Ads?

To manage and create an audience in Facebook ads, you will have to use the Audience Manager tool on Facebook. This tool can be found in the Business Manager by simply clicking on the top-right menu and choosing 'Audiences.'

Once the Audiences page opens up, you can view all your

previously saved Facebook audiences and also have the option to build a new one. To completely understand the broad range of targeting options available on Facebook ads, we must begin from the basics.

Audiences in Facebook ads are primarily of three types:

- Saved Audiences
- Lookalike Audiences
- Custom Audiences

Each of these audience categories gives you ample options for building the perfect target audience for your Facebook ads campaign. Let's take a more in-depth look into each of these types:

Facebook Saved Audiences

Saved audiences on Facebook are the audiences that can be defined by choosing their interests, age, location, gender, income level, used devices, etc. You can build a saved audience in both the Audience Manager and the marketing campaign setup stage.

Facebook Custom Audiences

Custom audiences on Facebook are most likely your highest-vale target audience as they allow you to retarget people who have previously engaged with your app or content and also past website visitors.

How to Create Custom Audiences on Facebook Ads?

There are several ways to create custom audiences on Facebook, and we are going to go through each briefly:

Creating a Custom Audience from Customer Files

This first kind of custom audience on Facebook is grounded on your existing customer files – phone numbers, Apple IDs, and a list of email accounts. The customer file audiences are an excellent way to target your app users or newsletter subscribers.

To create a Custom Audience on Facebook, follow these instructions:

- Click on the 'Customer File' option.
- Pick whether you want to import contacts from Mailchimp or Wish to add a customer file.
- Import the customer data to generate a new Custom Audience.
- Choose identifiers.
- Upload a customer file.
- Give the Custom Audience a name/title.

Customer files can involve fifteen varying identifiers; the most popular ones are phone number, email, and mobile advertiser ID.

We'll cover this more in-depth in the next chapter.

Creating a Custom Audience from Website Traffic

Creating a custom audience from website traffic allows you to build a remarketing campaign for individuals who have previously engaged with your webpage. These audiences are of high significance as they have shown interest in your Facebook ads in the past.

To create a custom audience based on your webpage traffic, you must first install the Facebook Pixel. Check out our blog section for a complete guide on what it is and how it works. Once the Facebook Pixel is installed, you can head to the Audience Manager and build a custom audience on your past website traffic. You have the option to choose between numerous preferences:

- Target everybody who visited your website.
- Target individuals who have visited particular web pages.
- Target individuals who have visited certain web pages but not the rest.
- Target individuals who have not been to your website for a specific amount of time.

You also have several other custom combination options available.

Creating a Custom Audience Based on App Activity

If you wish to reach the individuals who have engaged with your Android or iOS app, you can easily set up a Facebook target audience for this job. But first, you must register your app and set up app events to target individuals based on the app activity.

To build a Facebook Custom Audience grounded on your app activity, target folks who have taken particular actions or events in your app. Time frames can also be selected for targeted events. For instance, you can select a purchase event and choose 'in the last 600 days' option to reach individuals who have accomplished an in-app purchase event in the last sixty days.

Creating a Custom Audience Based on Customer Engagement

Facebook ads also give you the option to target users that have previously engaged with your content on Facebook, for example, liked a post on your page or viewed your videos. The newest add-on to custom audiences is the opportunity to target individuals who have participated in one of the following actions:

- Visited your Facebook Page
- Clicked on a call-to-action (CTA) button
- Engaged with your ads or posts
- Saved your post or page
- Sent a message to your page

This provides you with the ideal opportunity to reach high-value audiences interested in learning more about your product or service and brand.

10 Sources to Use for Creating Your Custom Audience

1. Website Traffic (up to 180 days - if you've installed the Pixel)
2. App Activity (up to 180 days - if you've installed the Pixel)
3. Customer List
4. Offline Activity
5. Video (users who watched 3 or 10 seconds of your video within the last 365 days)
6. Lead Forms (Users who filled out or opened your lead form on Facebook in the last 90 days)
7. Instant Experience (Users who opened your Instant Experience ad AND who clicked any link in it in the last 365 days)

8. Instagram (Everyone who has engaged with your business on Instagram in the last 365 days)
9. Events (Users who RSVP'd as going or interested in the last 365 days)
10. Facebook Pages (Everyone who has engaged with your page in the last 365 days)

Facebook Lookalike Audiences

Lookalike audiences on Facebook allow you to reach individuals who are identical to your existing customer database and making increasing the chances of receiving conversions.

To produce a lookalike audience on Facebook, you must first build a Custom Audience to inform Facebook what kind of users you want to reach.

The next step is to choose the 'Lookalike Audience' option from the audience creation menu and pick a target country and a percentage, 1 percent to 10 percent, of the selected country's Facebook users. The fraction indicates the individuals most related to your selected Custom Audience.

Facebook lookalike audiences allow you to amplify your ad campaigns reach and help you to target only those individuals who are most likely to be interested in your product or service.

How to Taper Your Facebook Audiences?

Often, a Facebook audience might include millions of people. Unless you have a myriad of dollars worth advertising budget waiting around the corner, you must keep the target audiences precise and smaller. Preferably, it should involve individuals that have the highest probability of converting through your marketing campaign.

When creating Saved Audiences, you can easily taper your audience with the or/and targeting options. The 'or' targeting option indicates that when you insert new targeting options in the same set of targeting, your target audience will grow bigger. On the other hand, the 'and' targeting option shows that an individual in your target audience should fall into numerous categories. This will allow you to create niche audiences and reduce the audience size.

In addition to this, you also have the option to exclude individuals who match particular demographics or interests. Moreover, you can omit certain custom audiences from your general target audience. For instance, you can exclude past converters to prevent your ads from reaching individuals who are already your customers.

By recognizing and targeting the right audience, you can be a game-changer to achieve high-value results through your Facebook ads and marketing campaign. Otherwise, all your money and efforts will be going down the drain, and you will be left with nothing but a flop marketing endeavor.

You're now ready to go out there and create your own custom audience!

Creating a Custom Audience Using Contact Information

When it comes to building your business, you know just how important lead generation is. Perhaps you've been working on building your list of potential leads/prospects to reach out to. Once you've built your list now, you need to decide between cold calling, social outreach, email outreach, etc.

Whatever method you're using to contact leads, why not follow that up with some strategic Facebook ads to continue to nurture the relationship - just try not to be spammy with them.

Defining Your Target Audience

Who are you targeting to? It's easy to fall in the trap of thinking that anyone could be a customer when, in fact, everyone is *not* your customer. Understanding that can help you really fine-tune your marketing efforts and zero in on the people who are most likely to purchase your product or service.

Creating a Facebook Audience

While many businesses tend to stick to "boosting" a post (and then wonder why they're not getting conversions), if this book has taught you nothing else, there are so many opportunities and possibilities beyond just boosting. Enhance your Return on Investment (ROI) by creating impactful ads that reach the right people.

We'll talk about boosting a post versus Facebook Ads towards the end of this book.

Notice we said the *right* people?

With a clear understanding of who your target audience is, you can now create your audience (i.e. the people you're targeting with your Facebook ads). There is a wide range of demographics you can choose from to help you reach the right people, though we've already talked about this.

Here's what you may not know…

Your audience doesn't have to be limited to the individuals who fit the demographics you're targeting. You also have the option to target individuals who have been caught in your website's pixel (if you've installed it), create lookalike audiences, and even create an audience using contact information such as phone numbers and email addresses.

While we've already covered the basics of selecting demographics, so we'll move on to some other types of audiences.

Facebook Pixel

If you've installed the Facebook Pixel on your website, you have the ability to target everyone who has visited your website within the last X amount of days. If you have an ongoing campaign to drive traffic to your website, retargeting those that have visited your website with follow up ads could be a great way to getting that sales lead into your sales funnel.

From here, you also have the ability to create a "look-alike" audience based on who has visited your website. The people who visited your website likely have something in common. The Facebook algorithm looks for that commonality in similar users and will display your ad to those who have similar attributes to those who visited your website.

For more information on the Facebook Pixel, refer back to the previous chapter covering this topic.

Creating Audiences with Contact Information

Up until this point, we've talked about using Facebook Business Manager and Ads Manager to create your ads and determine your audience. However, you also have the availability to create ads using only an individual's contact information, such as their phone number or email address. You'll need to have your information ready to go for this step. So, let's walk through how to create an audience using only the lead's contact information.

There are two ways to create an audience with contact information. The first (and easiest way in this author's opinion) is through the "Leads Center" on your business page. If you don't have that option on your page, don't worry. Facebook states that it is only available on desktop computers to advertisers who have run campaigns with the *lead generation* objective in Ads Manager. If you fall into the category of *not* having this option, feel free to skip ahead.

Leads Center

From the "Leads Center," you have the ability to enter leads one at a time or even bulk upload a list from an excel document. From here, you'll also be able to track and categorize your leads with organizational features such as setting reminders to follow up, assigning an owner, adding notes,

The first thing you'll need to do is click on "Leads Center" from your business page.

Figure-34

Once the page has loaded, click on "Add Leads," which will show you two options to choose from: Create Lead and Upload Leads. If you choose the Create Lead, you'll be manually inputting leads one at a time. If you select Upload Leads, you can bulk upload your leads into the system.

Bulk Upload

When choosing to bulk upload your leads, you have the option to download the template format to use for uploading. If you're all set, go ahead and click on Choose File to upload your contacts. You'll be directed through a series of prompts. Once you've finished uploading, you'll need to refresh your screen to see your leads.

If you've bulk uploaded and your document wasn't formatted properly, your screen may appear like this:

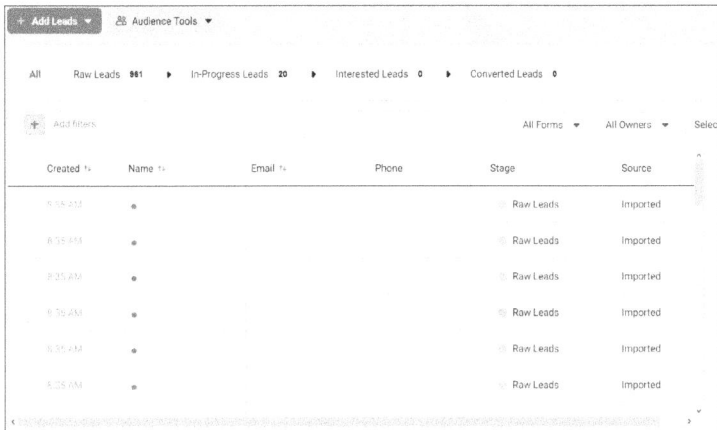

Figure-35

Despite its appearance, the leads are definitely in there. If you'd like to use the notes portion, you'll want to delete those and upload them again to get the formatting correct. After you've uploaded your leads, even if it looks like the screenshot above, you can then create your custom audience by clicking on "Audience Tools" and then "Create Custom Audience."

At this stage, you should already have set up your business manager and ad manager accounts and have your ad account linked. You'll need to select the appropriate ad account and give it a name. Now, from here, you'll want to either select "Raw Leads" meaning everyone you've just uploaded, "Converted Leads" (i.e. leads you've marked as converted to customers) or "other leads" in which you can individually select leads and not lump them all in together. Once you've finished, hit the preview button.

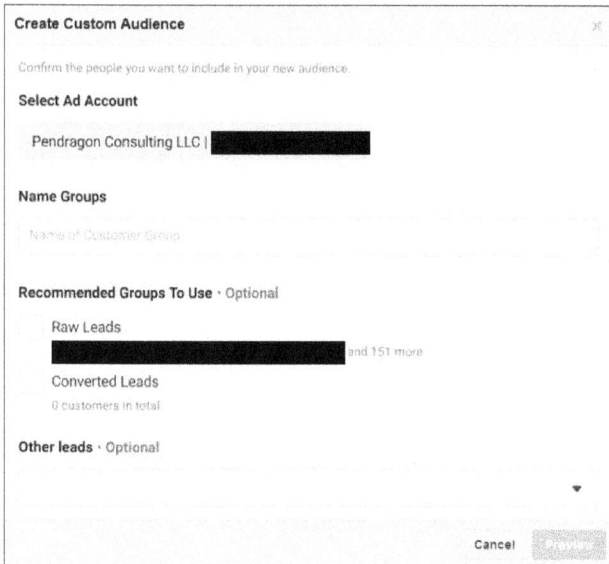

Figure-36

Once you've clicked preview, it will show you the list of leads that you'll be using to create your custom audience. Once you click on Create, it may ask you to agree to the terms and conditions before saving.

Manual Upload

If you're uploading manually by clicking Create Lead, you'll be prompted to enter the lead's information, similar to the form below.

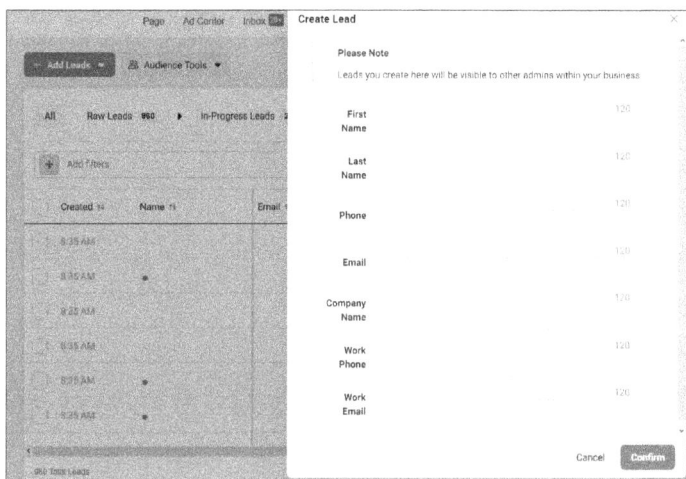

Figure-37

Once you've populated that data, you'll be able to see them appear in your list of raw leads. And boom - that's how you create a new lead entry for each individual.

Creating a Lookalike Audience Based on Leads

Get the most out of your list by creating a lookalike audience based on the leads you've uploaded by clicking on Audience Tools and selecting Create Lookalike Audience.

Similar to when you uploaded your leads, you'll have to enter some more information. Once you've selected the ad account, you'll be using a few more fields that will populate on the form, such as the Audience Location and Size.

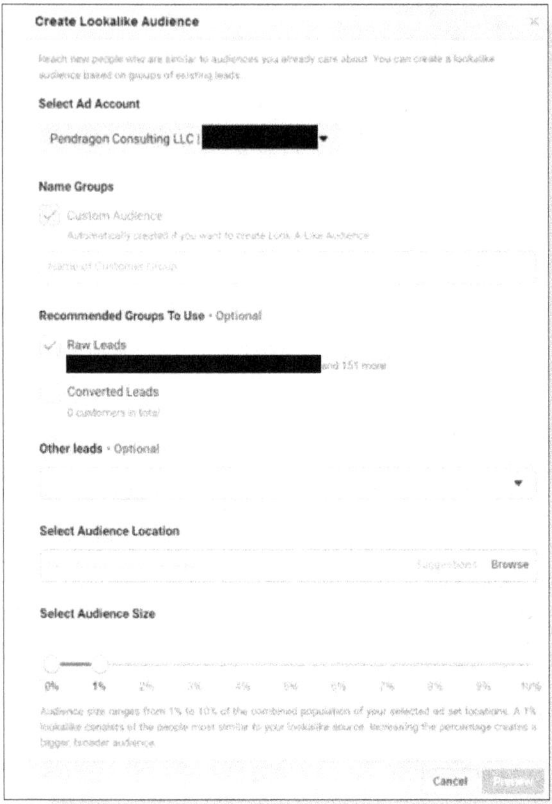

Figure-38

Again, once you've filled out the appropriate information, click on preview and then create to make your lookalike audience.

Easy peasy, right?

Ads Manager

If you don't have the option to upload and create your

audience through "Lead Forms" on your business page, you'll want to go to your Ads Manager account. From your Business Manager page, you can click on Audiences. This will open a new page where you'll be able to create and manage your various audiences. Once the page has loaded, you'll want to click on Create Audience, followed by Custom Audience. A popup will open that looks similar to this:

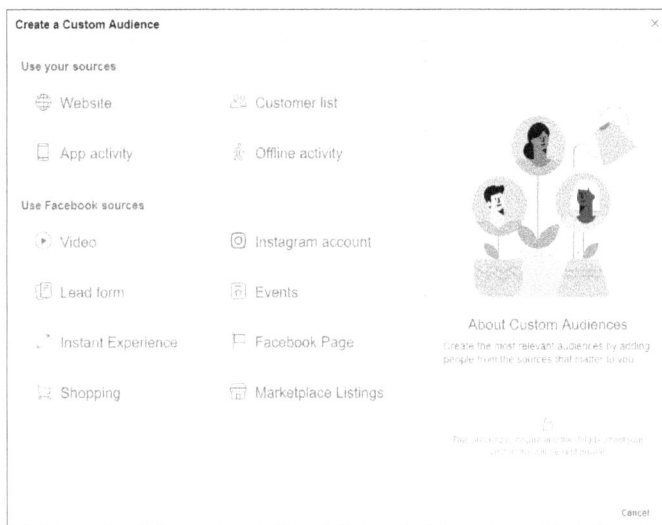

Figure-39

As you can see, there are many different ways that you can reach your target audience. For now, let's focus on the task at hand, uploading your leads to create a custom audience. To achieve that, you'll want to click on the Customer List.

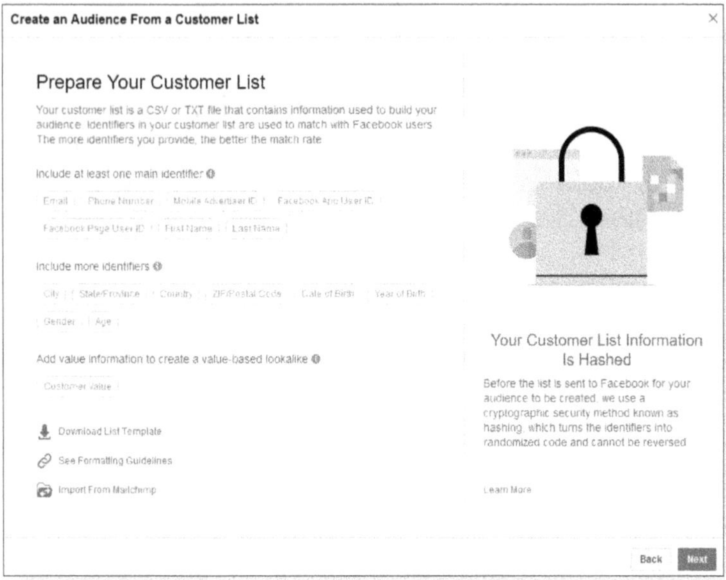

Figure-40

You'll want to have your leads loaded into either an XLS (excel) file or a TEXT file to upload them. Select the identifiers your list will include - such as email, phone number, first name, etc. When creating a list through this method, you're also able to identify the most valuable leads so that when you create a lookalike audience, it is modeled after those that are deemed most valuable and not just ladi-dadi-everybody. For those using Mailchimp, you also have the option to import directly from your Mailchimp account, making it even easier.

Similar to the Leads Center method, from there, you'll simply upload your leads and name your audience.

Once you've successfully added your list, it will

automatically give you the option to create a lookalike audience.

That's it. Now, when you go to run an ad on Facebook, you'll have audiences that will help improve your lead nurturing and Return on Investment (ROI).

Jessica Ainsworth

Optimize Your ROI with These Pro Tips

There's always more to everything than meets the eye, including Facebook Advertising. There are a number of different tips and tricks to really maximize your ROI and increase conversions. Two of those methods are dayparting and the stockpile method. Read on to learn more about each of those and how they can benefit your ad campaigns.

Dayparting

Want to make sure that your ads are being displayed when your followers are actually online? Consider dayparting your ad campaigns.

What is Dayparting?

Dayparting is the practice of scheduling your ad campaigns to run only at certain times, on certain days, so your ads are being shown to your followers and potential customers *when they're actually online*. Yet another feature, often underutilized, that can help you optimize your advertisements and increase your ROI.

Here's what you need to understand and combing through your Insights can help you with this next process. There are going to be certain hours that your audience will be most likely to *see* your ad, certain hours in which your audience is more likely to *click, engage, or convert*, and while there will be some time overlap for many, others will find that there is no overlap.

There is no one-size-fits-all optimal time. You'll need to do your homework on this one - or try split testing. Determining your optimal timing and dayparting your ads can help you improve your conversion rate, reduce wasted click and produce a higher ROI.

Dayparting can also make sure that your audience never sees the same ad twice.

Using Facebook Insights to Determine Optimal Times

As we mentioned above, you can use your page's Insights to determine optimal days and times for posting. You can do this by clicking on the "Insights" tab at the top of your Facebook business page. On the left-side menu, click on "posts," and you'll see something like this:

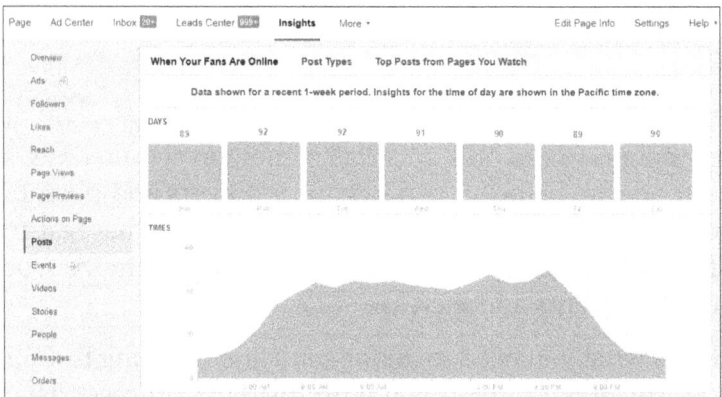

Figure-41

As you can see from this visual, the data covering this 7-day window indicate that this page's followers are all online pretty consistently each day of the week. However, from the times that this page's followers are online, it appears that our optimal window is from 3 pm - 6 pm. From here, we can also identify that from 10 pm - about 5 am, the number of followers online decreases pretty dramatically. This means that having our advertisements displayed between 10 pm - 5 am wouldn't be very effective for our ROI.

Armed with the knowledge of how to identify when would be optimal for advertising, you are now ready to head over to Facebook Business Manager and daypart your ad.

Setting Up a Dayparting Campaign Schedule in Ads Manager

At this stage, we've walked through a step by step process to create an advertisement in Facebook Ads Manager. Once you've selected your objective, targeting and placements as you normally would, you'll see the "budget & schedule" section. In order to be able to set up your dayparting schedule, you'll need to select a *lifetime budget* instead of a daily budget. Once you've selected a *lifetime budget,* you'll then be given two options: 1) Run ads all the time and 2) Run ads on a schedule. You'll need to select *Run ads on a schedule.*

From here you'll be able to choose the days and times that you'd like your advertisement to show.

Stockpiling Ads

Do you remember our earlier mention of how only about 1.6 - 2% of your followers will see your *organic* posts depending on the level of engagement? The more people that engage with your post, the more that Facebook will show your post on, in this case, ad. Facebook's advertising algorithm favors ads that are deemed valuable to the platform's users. Hence, the more engagement your post has (likes, comments, shares, etc.), the more the algorithm determines your post to be valuable and therefore, the more your post will be shown. For this reason, some advertisers will go the route of stockpiling ads.

The Stockpile Method is where an advertiser uses a preexisting post or advertisement that had a decent level of engagement on it and reruns the campaign.

Each time you duplicate or edit an ad, Facebook erases all engagement, which can harm your ad's performance and, therefore, results.

How to Use the Stockpile Method

Using the stockpile method is both easy and effective. Go ahead and enter the information required for the campaign, ad set and ad level. Once you've completed that, go back into your ad level and click "Ad Preview," followed by "See Post - Facebook with Comments." Now, you'll need to copy the post ID, which is a 15-digit number that appears on the URL of your advertisement.

Lastly, create a new ad using the post ID that you've just copied.

By using this method, you're able to copy over the original ad and keep all of the engagement the original post built up.

Go on, optimize your next campaign and watch the ROI rack up.

Using Facebook Audience Insights for Precise Ad Targeting

Facebook, despite being less popular with millennial and Gen Z users, is going strong in terms of businesses using it as a platform for reaching out to masses of their audience. The social media Goliath continues to hold the popularity reigns as more than 1.73 billion active users log on to the platform daily.

The saturation of users on the platform is one reason why many brands use it; a sizable portion of their target market is likely on Facebook. The opportunities and outreach for advertisements are significant just on the platform.

As it is with every marketing campaign, whether conventional or digital, one has to be sure that the advertisement and other messages are reaching their audience.

So how does a digital marketer know that they are targeting the right people, whether it's actually generating the results they were expecting, and how they can use the data to further streamline and increase the effectiveness of their Facebook ads?

The answer is in three words:

Facebook. Audience. Insights.

Facebook Audience Insights

If you boil it down to basics, Facebook Audience Insights or FAI is a tool Facebook provides for businesses to use. It shows information about the people that follow or like your page, the people defined in your custom audience, and the aggregate of all the people on the platform.

You can find the tool in the Facebook Ads Manager. Here's how you can use is to extract meaningful information out of the tool and then use it to rejuvenate your advertisement campaigns and facilitate the generation of results that affect your business positively.

Step 1: Getting Started

The first step in using FAI is choosing the insights you want to see and work with. When you click and open the FAI dashboard, a pop up will open, asking you to choose the audience you want to start with.

If you are a social media manager working multiple accounts, you can choose the right one on the right-hand corner where it shows your accounts.

Typically, you will get two options:

1. Everyone on Facebook
2. People connected to your page

If you have previously customized an audience, you will get that as the third option. You can choose either one, but as this brief guide is directed at those who are new to this venture, we will work with the first option (Everyone on Facebook).

Step 2: Getting the Audience Demographics Right

The next step essentially involves building a new audience. This helps narrow down the silos of data Facebook has in store. Click on the Demographics tab. On the left-hand side, you will see filters that are different demographics; you can select to see the trends change on the graphs present on the main panel.

You will see the following options:

- Location
- Age and Gender
- Interests

The first two are pretty straightforward, but it's the *interests* section that is... well, interesting. You begin with a broad umbrella interest that is basically your area of business. For instance, if you were in the business of selling apparel, you would choose clothing and then further narrow down.

Facebook has designed its platform and algorithms in a way that it lets you fidget and dig deeper. Advanced demographics include relationship status, education level, language, job titles, etc.

By tuning your audience metrics and making them more precise, you remove vagueness that would keep you from targeting specific people with very specific content.

Step 3: What Do They Like?

You now have an audience that you want to cater to. With that information, you can further get into the nitty-gritty of your audience and see what their interests converge.

In this section, you are basically observing what categories of pages they like. For example, you will get 10 categories based on your audience, determining the types of pages that are most popular within your targeted audience.

In addition to categories, you can see the names of the exact pages your audience likes. Relevance and Affinity of each page, which combinedly determine the relevancy of the page for your audience and the likelihood of them liking or following it.

You can use these to test your demographics and see if it affects the results.

Step 4: Going Further Down the Line

After the Demographics and Page Like tabs, it's time to venture into and dig around the *Locations* tab. This is extremely important for all those businesses that rely on their location for their online sales.

For brick and mortar companies, the location is fixed. But for online businesses, this tab will reveal which countries and cities they should target along with languages. For example, if you type in anime cosplay outfits, you can see which countries collectively have more people interested.

With this information, you can hyper-target your audience based on where they are located. The language information will help with translations and making information available in languages that a significant segment of your target audience speaks.

For example, K-Pop or Korean pop music is a big hit in the US and around Europe: i.e. English-speaking countries besides Korea. This is why when K-pop artists now release music, they have English subtitles. Some songs even feature words or complete verses in English.

Step 5: Activity Details

The fourth and last tab on the FAI dashboard is the Activity Tab. Under this tab, you can see where your audience accesses Facebook and how they spend their time.

If you look at the date of your target audience's primary devices, the chart will show the percentage of desktop-only and mobile users. Mobile users are then further broken down into Android, computer (laptop), iPad, iPhone, Blackberry etc.

The Final Call – The Ads

At the end of thoroughly playing around and studying your target audience's demographics, likes, usage metrics, etc., you will have a clearer picture of what you need to do to generate better engagement on your targeted ads.

If this deep dive into the insights drives a number north of 1000 in your target audience, go ahead and craft an ad targeted at them. On the same dashboard, there is a Create Ad button you can click on to build an ad using the audience you have saved.

We have discussed in detail about using Facebook Ads Manager for creating and targeting ads. If you haven't, we suggest that you do a little homework, or you can simply follow the guidelines that Facebook will prompt when you switch to the ad creator dashboard.

Don't forget to set tracking metrics and actively follow them up after posting the ad and running A/B tests prior.

Remarketing

Have you ever visited a company's website, and then all of a sudden, you were seeing ads for them everywhere? That's an example of remarketing. If you've seen those ads on Facebook, then you've been caught by the company's Facebook pixel, and they are using the social platform to remarket to you. Read on.

When people are shopping around, they may leave without purchasing anything (aka abandoned cart). If you're selling services over products, then you may want visitors to fill out a form or click "call now" to convert hopefully, but instead, they click away. Now what? How will you reel them back in? Sometimes, people want to shop around before committing to anything, but you can help inspire them to come back to your website by remarketing to them.

Remarketing is a term used to describe advertising that targets people who have previously visited your website and is accomplished with the help of Facebook's Pixel.

The first step to remarketing involves installing the Facebook Pixel code on your website. The Facebook Pixel, if you remember, allows you to track your website visitors and keep your brand fresh in their minds when you remarket to them.

Remember that with all ads - remarketing included - you need to make sure that your ads are tailored to your audience. If you're remarketing to people who visited your website, understanding why they visited your website in the first place can help you create a more impactful ad.

Example

Let's say that you've just spent $X on driving traffic to your website using Facebook Ads. From that, let's say you got 50 unique link clicks to your website. That's 50 potential customers right there. And now that you've spent that money on bringing them to your website and capturing them in your pixel, now's the chance to remarket to them and reel them back in.

Pro-Tip

Keep an eye on your Pixel's insights and your Google Analytics to keep you informed on how many visitors you're getting and when. You can daypart your remarketing ads to when your website drives the most traffic to really maximize your ROI.

Split Testing

When you create an ad campaign across your Facebook family of apps and services, the campaign's success relies heavily on multiple variables.

The only accurate way to know whether your ad is performing at peak efficiency or not is by testing several iterations of the same advertisement. This process is known as split testing. This ad performance analysis technique can be wearisome at times, particularly if you are unfamiliar with Facebook Ads.

But don't worry, we've got your back!

In this chapter, we'll uncover everything you need to know about split testing in Facebook ads and provide you with a complete guide to split test all aspects of your ad campaign to improve its ROI significantly.

What is Split Testing?

Split testing, also known as the A/B test, is a marketing strategy where two variables of an ad campaign are tested against each other to evaluate and determine which one delivers the best results. It can be applied to almost everything you can think of, including blog post titles, emails, landing pages, and of course, Facebook ads.

A decent split test can result in considerable ROI improvements and increase the success result in up to 10 times! Everything can be analyzed in a split test, and even the variables that may seem insignificant can drastically improve your marketing performance.

Examples of Common Split Tests

Here are a few examples of the most common split tests:

- Images or videos.
- Call to actions (Count me in vs. Sign Up).
- Audience targeting (age, gender, location)
- Color of critical elements such as the 'call to action' button.
- Element positioning (sign up form on the right or left side of the page)

Why is Split Testing Important?

Split testing ensures that important decisions are not made based on a mere gut feeling or guesswork.

Without split testing, people often create changes based on past best practices or the highest-paid person's opinion (HiPPO). But they do not realize that best practices can kill conversions, as, by definition, they are grounded on what worked in the past for others; but there is no guarantee that what worked for them would also work for you. Similarly, the highest-paid person's opinion can also be just as flawed as anyone else's.

Experienced marketers, copywriters, and designers can even prove to be wrong while trying to figure out what the audience will respond to. Thus, split testing allows optimization teams to determine which route to take and prevents them from going down a dead end.

Benefits of Split Testing

Most marketers conduct a split test because they suspect a facet of their marketing campaign is not working well, or they believe better results can be achieved. There are several potential benefits offered by split testing; few of these include:

- Eliminating guesswork and getting rid of any uncertainty related to the marketing campaign.
- Discovering how the target audience actually responds, rather than mere assumptions that can happen with survey data.
- Acquiring crucial insights that can drive improvements.
- Creating more productive and better content.
- Optimizing web traffic and visitor engagement.
- Testing changes to reduce risks before making them permanent.
- Improves overall ROI.
- An easy and cost-effective way to improve marketing campaigns.

How to Run a Split Test?

There are numerous ways to run a split test on Facebook, depending on the variable you are trying to assess and where you create the A/B test. Usually, split testing is created through the Ads Manager toolbar on Facebook, making an existing ad campaign a template for your test.

Read ahead to know how this toolbar is used to create a split test:

- Click the 'Ads Manager' button to view the list of all

your existing ad campaigns.

- To create the new split test, click the box present on the left side of the ad campaign(s) you'd like to use as a template.
- Click the 'A/B Test' option present on top of the toolbar.
- Choose your desired variable and follow the on-screen instructions.

In addition to this, you can create a split test **by duplicating an existing ad, campaign, or ad set** present in the Ads Manager to modify a current ad and compare performance quickly. This allows you to alter one or more elements of the strategy and determine which one performs better. Moreover, it helps you choose a variable and guides you through several potential changes that can lead to the development of a winning ad strategy.

Facebook Split Testing Best Practices

Make sure to keep these best practices in mind before you start your split test. These will help you to conduct tests that are applicable and valuable for your next ad campaign on Facebook.

1. Select one variable that will help you reach your ultimate goal as results are more conclusive this way.
2. Pick a new audience that you'd like to reach through the ad. Make sure that it is large enough to produce measurable results.
3. Use hypotheses that are valuable and measurable. Moreover, ensure that your hypothesis is easy to understand, clear, and possible to be determined through a split test.

4. To receive accurate and meaningful results, set up time frames that are ideal and capable of producing enough data for valuable findings.
5. Develop a budget for the split test that works best for your business. This can help you to establish a winning strategy while keeping costs into consideration.

The Giveaway

Hands down, split testing on Facebook Ads is one of the most successful ways to improve your ad performance and generate a better ROI significantly. It can also help marketers better understand who their customers are and what these customers truly want from the business.

Jessica Ainsworth

Troubleshooting

Because when there's something strange in your Facebook Ads, who are you going to call? (Did you get my Ghostbusters reference there?!)

Here are a few troubleshooting tips, so you don't *actually* have to call someone.

Three of the most common issues you may encounter on your Facebook Advertising journey are:

• Ads are disapproved
• Ads get stuck in review
• Ad account is disabled

Ads Are Disapproved

Welcome to the club. There's nothing more frustrating than to wait 24 hours for your ad to come back as disapproved. While there is a chance that your ad was mistakenly disapproved (in which case you can request a manual review), more often than not, your ad was rejected as a result of it violating Facebook's Ad Policy. Remember, they can reject your ad for something as minor as grammatical issues. When your ads are disapproved, Facebook will let you know which part of your ad violated Facebook's policy. After you've fixed your ad, you can then resubmit your ad. If you feel that your ad falls into a gray area, you can always request a manual review of your ad.

Ads Stuck in Review

Once you've finished creating your ad, Facebook must

review it and approve it before it is published.   This process can take up to 48 hours for your ad to be approved, though there are instances in which it can take longer for Facebook to review your ad(s). For instance, if your account is new, it may take a bit longer for Facebook to approve your ad. If you find that your ad is taking longer than normal in the review stage, outside of contacting Facebook's support team, there are two main ways to fix this:

1. Request Manual Review
2. Duplicate the Ad and Publish

Ad Account is Disapproved

Reasons your ad account may be disabled include violations of Facebook's Ad policy or if it has been flagged for unusual activity.

If you believe that your ad account was disabled by mistake, you can request a review of your restricted ad account by visiting:

https://www.facebook.com/help/contact/2026068680760273

Request Review of Restricted Ad Account

If your ad account was disabled because it didn't comply with our Advertising Policies or other standards, you can request a review if you believe it shouldn't be disabled. Please note that due to coronavirus (COVID-19) we have fewer people available for reviews and it may take several weeks to get a response

Is this your account?

Yes

No

Send

Figure-42

If you've received a notification that your account has been flagged for unusual activity, you'll need to fill out a form here to file an appeal:

https://www.facebook.com/help/contact/ 391647094929792

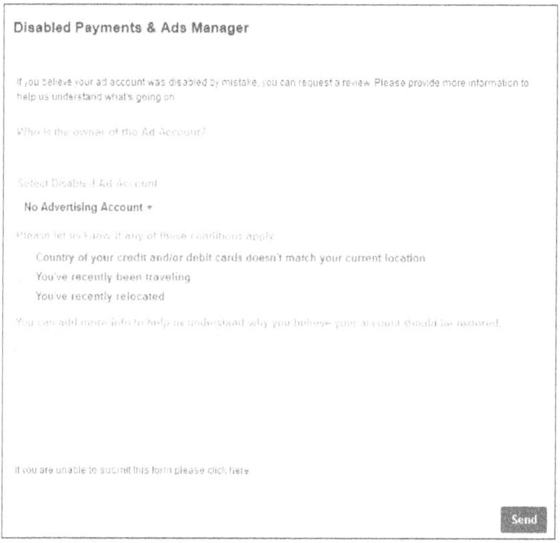

Disabled Payments & Ads Manager

If you believe your ad account was disabled by mistake, you can request a review. Please provide more information to help us understand what's going on.

Who is the owner of the Ad Account?

Select Disabled Ad Account

No Advertising Account ▾

Please let us know if any of these conditions apply:

Country of your credit and/or debit cards doesn't match your current location

You've recently been traveling

You've recently relocated

You can add more info to help us understand why you believe your ad account should be restored.

If you are unable to submit this form please click here.

Send

Figure-43

Boosted Post v. Facebook Ads: What's the Difference?

Determining which method of advertising is right for you comes down to defining your advertising goals.

What is a Boosted Post?

When you post on your Facebook Business page, it appears as a post on your timeline. On most of those posts, you'll see the option to Boost it. But what is that? While both Boosting a post and Facebook Ads are forms of advertising and can help you reach a larger audience, they both have different objectives they accomplish.

Boosting a post is the easiest way for advertisers to get their name out there as it does not require you to use Business Manager, which can seem pretty intimidating to those who don't know how to use it.

A boosted post lets you show a post you've created and posted to your Business's timeline to people who may not already follow your page. Of course, if your objective is to make sure a larger number of your followers are seeing your advertisement, you can always select to target those who are already followers.

Your boosted post will show up in your audience's News Feed as an advertisement, and you can choose whether you'd like it displayed on Facebook or Instagram.

Brand awareness is the main objective of boosting a post and is not generally good for lead generation or conversion purposes. By boosting a post, you can increase the number of likes, shares, comments and build your brand visibility.

What is a Facebook Ad?

Facebook Ads are created through your Ads Manager account in Business Manager. Whereas boosting a post can help you build brand awareness, creating an ad in Ads Manager allows you to optimize your ad for app installs, website conversions, video views, shop order, lead generation and much more.

You'll also have more flexibility in where your ads can be shown. When boosting a post, you're limited to having your post shown to your audience on Facebook and/or Instagram, on your audience's News Feed. When advertising through Ads Manager, you open up a wider range of possibilities such as their Audience Network (off of Facebook), Messenger, Instant Articles, Stories, Instagram, Facebook, etc.

You can also choose your objective as there's so much more than just building brand awareness. Drive visitors to your website, generate qualified leads, local business promotions and more.

In creating a Facebook Ad through Ads Manager, you have access to advanced targeting capabilities. In addition to being able to select demographics such as age, gender, location, interests, etc., you can also create custom audiences with that information, lookalike audiences and even audiences based off of your existing contact information you have for your prospective clients.

Determining Your Objective

If your objective is to simply build brand awareness, then boosting a post may be the right course of action for you.

If you're looking for a way to really dive in and reach new pools of potential clients, creating a Facebook Ad in Ads Manager is where you want to be.

Facebook Page versus Facebook Group

Social media has changed the way businesses function and carry out their operations. It connects people faster than ever before, irrespective of their location and in a previously unimaginable way.

Customer communication, direct feedback, reviews, and complaints – social media offers a platform to attain it all and more efficiently.

Facebook is one of those platforms that provide optimal benefits to brands if used effectively and in the right way. But with all of its current and emerging features, it can be a tough task to decide which Facebook tool to use for your brand.

Facebook groups and pages being the two tools highlighted in this article. But which out of the two is most lucrative for brand promotion? Facebook group, or Facebook page?

Before you decide, let's take a look at both to ascertain, which is more rewarding for your brand.

Facebook Page for Brands

A Facebook page similar to the individual profiles of Facebook users, the significant difference being that it is essentially a page dedicated to brands, celebrities, businesses, and organizations. It comprises of several business-friendly features. Few of which are:

• Brands can easily access information about the performance of the page through page insights. User demographics data can also be attained through this

feature.
- Admins can assign tasks to other individuals who have access to the page.
- Access to third-party apps can enhance the experience for visitors to the page.
- CTA's can be created by brands on the page to accomplish business goals.
- Tabs can be used to navigate visitors and highlight relevant sections.

Additionally, there are several benefits offered by a Facebook page.

- **Organic Reach and Credibility**: As Facebook pages can show up in search engines like Google because they're public, this can increase the organic reach of a brand and strengthen its credibility.
- **Display Brand Personality**: Facebook pages are a great way to showcase a brand's personality or business through the content generated and posted on the page. The first thing people nowadays do before they make a purchase is to learn about the product or service from its page. Thus, having a page dedicated to a brand is the best thing to do for their business.
- **Platform to Broadcast Information**: Brand pages on Facebook are an excellent tool for broadcasting promotional material or sharing business-related news. Moreover, it is also a great platform to interact with large groups of the target audience.

Facebook Group for Brands

Facebook groups are more of a coming together point for

individuals around a cause. The cause could be anything from brand promotion, public issue awareness, or selling and buying things. Anyone can make a Facebook group and join several groups that interest them. (Don't forget to join our Facebook group for some helpful tips on Facebook Advertising!) Some features of a Facebook group include:

- Group members can interact with each other and hold discussions
- Hold live video sessions to create awareness about an issue or sell a product
- Facebook groups can be private, public, or even secret, depending on who the brand wants to target.

Some broad benefits of Facebook groups are:

1. **Fosters Community Feeling**: The significant advantage of having a Facebook group is that it encourages and fosters a feeling of togetherness as people can directly communicate and engage with each other.
2. **Economic Activity**: Another key benefit of having a Facebook group is that people can easily use the platform to sell their products or services without setting up a virtual shop. This is especially beneficial for small-scale brands or startups.

Facebook Page v. Facebook Group – Which is Better for Your Brand?

The answer to this question can solely be determined by the purpose or goal your brand wants to accomplish.

If you are seeking to promote and establish your brand, having a Facebook page makes the most sense. On the other hand, if you are a small-scale business or a new startup, creating a Facebook group can help you establish a presence and personal engagement.

Although a group can be an add-on that drives traffic to your page, thus having a dedicated page is what a brand needs more.

On the Horizon: New Features Coming Soon

Just as we are continuing to grow and change, so too is the technology and the Facebook platform. In addition to the usual algorithm updates, there are normally some new features that get rolled out to us lowly mortals after beta testing. So, what are some of those snazzy features on the horizon?

• Facebook Collections
• Advertising in Facebook Groups

Read on to learn more…

Making Facebook Collections Work for Your Business

Have you ever saw a recipe, a funny photo, an article you want to read, but just don't have the time on Facebook and wished you could save it for later? Well, you actually can. It turns out not many people know about this function, but users have the ability to go in and create collections of items. Facebook will be rolling out new capabilities soon that will allow users to make those collections public. Not sure how that might benefit your business? Read on.

What Are Facebook Collections?

Facebook Collections are just that - a collection of items that users have saved to a list. I can't tell you how many times I've run across a recipe or an article that I wanted to save for later but couldn't. You don't always have the time to read the articles or make the recipes the moment they cross your timeline. Enter Facebook Collections.

The feature allows users to do content curation in real-time, to save items they want to view later. And soon, they'll let you share those lists with yourself, contributors to your lists/collections, friends, or even to make them publicly available so anyone can see them.

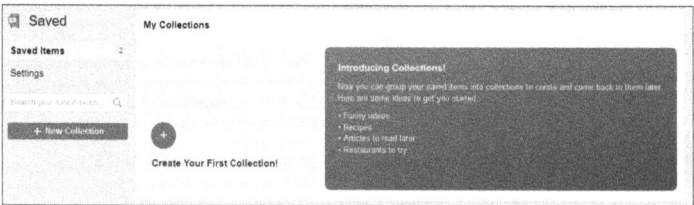

Figure-44

How to Save Content to a Collection

Let's say you come across a really interesting article written by one of your favorite bloggers (is it me?!), and you want to save the article to read it later. How would you go about doing this? Well, it's simple. See those three dots in the top right corner of the post? If you click on that, you'll see an option to "save link" or "save video, photo, etc." depending on the type of content.

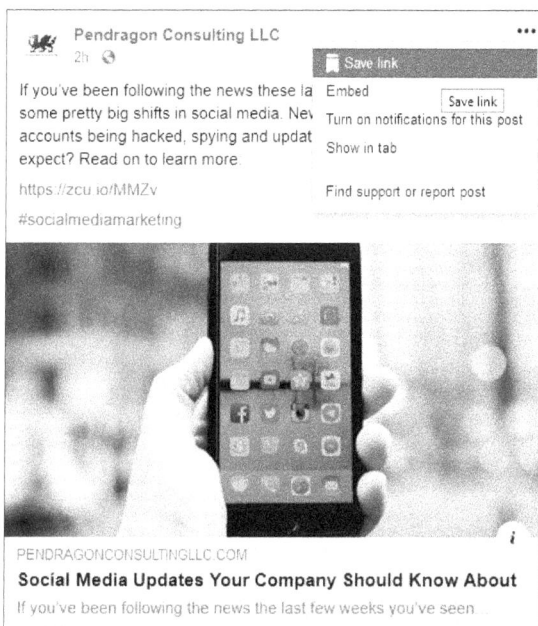

Figure-45

Once you've clicked on saving a link, you'll see the option at the top of the post to either view your saved items or to add the post to a collection. If you click "add to a collection," you'll have the ability to save it to a collection you've already created or to create a new collection.

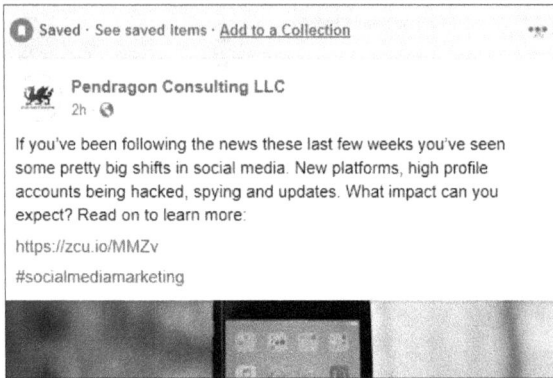

Figure-46

Alternatively, if you wanted to create the collection and then save items to it later, you can go to www.facebook.com/saved to create new collections as well as view, edit and delete current collections. Another option to access your collections is to click on "Saved" on the left side menu on your Facebook newsfeed.

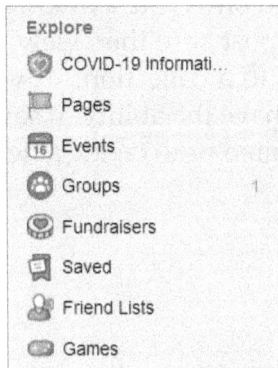

Figure-47

How Facebook Collections Can Benefit Businesses

I'm sure it's only a matter of time before Facebook offers businesses the ability to advertise in their collections. However, until they've formally released the ability to make the collections public, there's not much we can do but wait and start getting our content set up.

So, how can your company benefit from this feature? Exposure. There are a couple of directions that you could take this to really maximize your social media marketing on Facebook. First, consider working with a social media influencer to include your product, services, blog posts, etc. in their collections that they push out to their large followings. Second, work with community leaders on being included in any resources for local services, events, etc. to ensure your information is included in any collections they release. Finally, create your own content and once the ability to push the collection public is released, share, share, share.

If you're a real estate agent, this feature could be extremely beneficial to your social media marketing efforts. Create a list with some articles on your website offering tips on home buying, facts, statistics, photos of property listings, videos, etc. The trick to this, like most of your content, is to not be full salesy. Include information that will make people want to take notice of your collection. Provide information they'll find useful outside of just selling to them.

And this could really work for most industries. Financial advisors could put together a collection of items to help provide resources to those looking to prepare for retirement or even one for investment strategies, historical information, current events, etc. Again, provide information, photos, videos, etc. in your collections that will make users want to view and engage with your collections.

Experimental Phase

As of right now, Facebook is only testing the new sharing options (ability to share with the public) with a selected group of users in the United States. However, I think it's safe to say this is something worth keeping an eye on as it holds a lot of potential for reaching new audiences. Start getting your collections ready, and when the ability is released to the rest of Facebook's users, you can be ready to dominate the competition.

Advertising in Facebook Groups

Facebook Groups are valuable in and of themselves. Why not create a group on Facebook relevant to your industry? In these groups, you don't want to sell or spam your fellow Group members, but rather use it as a way to build connections and for those that have expressed interest, spread the word about your offerings.

However, at this stage, you're not able to advertise with a sponsored post in any Facebook Groups. These sponsored groups are paid advertisements and do not need to be approved by Group moderators.

Once this feature is out of beta testing and gets rolled out to the rest of us, you'll be able to opt whether you'd like your ads to appear in Facebook Groups in the "placements" section of your advertisement. If you leave your placement settings on "automatic placement," your ads will automatically determine which place makes the most sense, and your ad may, in fact, be shown in some Facebook Groups. If you select "manual placement," you'll be able to select each place you'd like your ad to show up - including Groups.

When running an ad in the Facebook Groups Feed, it will appear alongside other community posts in the mobile feed of the Group. Of note, this placement will only be available for "single image ads that use Reach, Off-site Conversions or Link Click objectives."

Keep your eyes open, folks! Big things are coming!

Jessica Ainsworth

Additional Resources

Free Resources

Download your free packet of templates, infographics and other resources by visiting:

www.beginnersguidetomarketing.com/facebookadvertising

Resources on Facebook

Facebook for Business -
https://www.facebook.com/business

This resource is Facebook's end all, be all of everything you need to know about Facebook and Facebook advertising. When querying for a particular issue, they will also link in there to other relevant articles as well as any contact information and/or forms to submit.

Facebook Learn -
https://www.facebook.com/business/learn

Facebook Learn offers you the ability to learn more and prepare for your Blueprint certifications. It teaches you all about advertising on Facebook.

Facebook Blueprint -
https://www.facebook.com/business/learn/certification

This is the link to take you to the Blueprint certification exams after you've utilized Facebook Learn to prepare for the test.

Facebook Ads Library -
https://www.facebook.com/ads/library/

Have a look through the Ads library to see what's working and what's not working to help shape your own ads.

Agency Hub -
https://www.facebook.com/business/m/fmp/agencies

Support for advertising agencies. Allows agencies to contact customer support, offers Blueprint resources and can sign up for agency events.

Facebook Ad Formats Guide -
https://www.facebook.com/business/ads-guide

Every ad placement will have different formats that work best. Learn more by reading up on it with this resource.

Facebook Groups -
https://www.facebook.com/groups/
FBAdvertisingForBeginners/

We all need a little extra help, which is why we've created a group dedicated to like-minded individuals helping each other out with Facebook Advertising tips, resources and strategies.

Other Resources

Canva -
www.canva.com

Create some stunning graphics using Canva for an affordable price.

InVideo -
www.invideo.io

Create supercharge videos to wow your audience within both an easy and affordable way.

Google Trends -
https://trends.google.com/trends

Knowing what's trending can help you stay ahead of the curve with your content creation and staying relevant to your audience.

Pendragon Consulting, LLC -
https://www.PendragonConsultingLLC.com/blog

Our awesome and fabulous website has a blog section that provides additional information and resources for Facebook advertisers and those looking to boost their marketing skills in general.

Precision Legal Marketing -
https://www.PrecisionLegalMarketing.com

A legal marketing agency based out of Virginia Beach, VA providing exceptional legal marketing to law firms around the nation. They also have a blog section chock full of useful information.

Jessica Ainsworth

Conclusion

There are more than 90 million small businesses using Facebook as a way of establishing an online presence. However, a good majority of them use regular Facebook pages or groups.

Facebook Business and Facebook Advertising can help these businesses further amplify their reach and build a more engaging and result-driving audience on the platform. It arms advertisers with tools that will work to the business's advantage.

Considering the self-reliance in terms of undertaking Facebook advertising on their shoulder, business owners must be well-versed with how it works. From setting up the Ad Manager for your page to creating a campaign, this guide was created with the prospect of helping first-timers.

With the information explained here, along with a solid strategy, you can create impactful ads, generate leads and increase revenue.

This book is meant to be a living document and a new version with all algorithm updates, tips and tricks will be available in 2021, so be on the lookout!

Let's Connect

We're always here to support our fellow businesses. Let's connect on social:

Facebook: https://www.facebook.com/ PendragonConsultingLLC/

LinkedIn: https://www.linkedin.com/company/ pendragon-consulting-llc

Twitter: https://twitter.com/LlcPendragon

Instagram: https://www.instagram.com/ pendragonconsultingllc/

YouTube: https://www.youtube.com/channel/ UCC6KY0eB5M-mLYNFWEUVtsw

We've also created a Facebook Group to help advertisers along their Facebook Advertising journey, so don't forget to join for some expert tips, tricks, strategies and valuable resources:

https://www.facebook.com/groups/ FBAdvertisingForBeginners/

Last mention - Keep in mind there are a number of free resources available for you to download on our website, free of charge to help you with your Facebook Advertising needs:

https://www.beginnersguidetomarketing.com/ facebookadvertising

About Pendragon Consulting

Your Partner in Expanding the Foregrounds of Digital Marketing Excellence

The story of digital marketing efficacy always starts with an effective strategy. Without a plan, you might as well be aimlessly targeting advertisements that lead to no results.

This is where Pendragon Consulting comes in. A strong penchant for research enables us to create that game plan and give you a strategy that will generate phenomenal results while also improving user engagement.

Who Is Pendragon Consulting?

Results-driven and research-focused, Pendragon Consulting, is a digital marketing agency helping businesses in the service industry gauge and optimize their online presence. We offer our clients a comprehensive range of digital marketing services that encompass our varying expertise.

We understand that your business deserves a stable online presence that delivers results. You put thought into the services you provide and the products you sell; so we put in the effort to make sure your efforts reach the right audience and gain you traction that improves your bottom line.

www.PendragonConsultingLLC.com

hello@pendragonconsultingllc.com

Author Bio

Jessica Ainsworth, Founder of Pendragon Consulting, LLC, a digital marketing agency based out of Maryland, is focused on helping businesses expand their reach into new pools of potential customers. She has a strong background in research and analytics and has turned that into a passion for marketing. Author of *The Beginner's Guide to Facebook Advertising: Create Impactful Ads and Increase Your Return on Investment* and *The Beginner's Guide to Content Marketing: How to Drive Traffic, Provide Value and Increase Revenue*, Jessica loves teaching small businesses how to stand on their own two feet to remain competitive without having to pay an agency to do it for them (unless they want to - in which case, give Pendragon a call).

Former intelligence analyst and total nerd, Jessica has a special fondness for research and analytics. Having a strong background in analytics, marketing seemed like an almost natural career transition. She is a veteran, author, marketing professional, philanthropist and board member at 22 March for Life, a veteran suicide prevention organization.

Connect with Jessica on LinkedIn!

LinkedIn personal: https://www.linkedin.com/in/jessica-ains-3b3194187/

Don't forget to join our Facebook Group: https://www.facebook.com/groups/FBAdvertisingForBeginners/